Cooking at Harmony Hill
Recipes for Hope and Healing

Fourth Edition, 2008

HARMONY
HILL
RETREAT CENTER

This book is lovingly dedicated to the thousands of cancer retreat participants who have found comfort and nourishment at Harmony Hill. May they be blessed on their journey towards healing.

Our deepest thanks to our fabulous cooks and inspired gardeners, past and present, whose loving intention makes all Harmony Hill food both wholesome and healing. Special thanks to Elaine Cook, author of our first cookbook, and to Elmer and Kitty Nordstrom, without whose enduring generosity Harmony Hill would not exist.

Cooking At Harmony Hill, 4th edition
Copyright © 2008 by Harmony Hill Retreat Center.
All rights reserved.

Printed in the United States of America.

Published and distributed by Harmony Hill Retreat Center,
7362 East State Route 106, Union, WA 98592.
Phone: (360) 898-2363. Email: info@harmonyhill.org.

Harmony Hill Retreat Center is a registered 501(c)(3) nonprofit organization. All proceeds from the sale of this cookbook directly benefit the Harmony Hill Cancer Retreat Program. To make a donation, or for more information, visit **www.harmonyhill.org**.

Text by Ann Lovejoy
Editing, design, and production by Anne Seeley
Design and production support from Linda Campbell
Cover photo @ 2008 by Victrinia Ensor

Our heartfelt thanks to the many Harmony Hill retreat participants whose kind words season the pages of this book.

CONTENTS

Foreword

Thank you for your generous support of Harmony Hill!

The purchase of this cookbook directly supports our cancer retreat program, which helps people find support, meaning, and creative coping strategies while facing the challenges of cancer. As this long-awaited fourth edition of our cookbook goes to press, we are celebrating Harmony Hill's 22nd anniversary as an organization and we are filled with gratitude for all that has unfolded here.

Harmony Hill's mission is to improve the quality of life for those affected by cancer, providing nurturing and resources that inspire renewal. To fulfill our mission, we offer retreat participants a dynamic, life-transforming experience, generous hospitality, and excellent service in the spectacular natural setting you see on the book's cover.

Harmony Hill is the Pacific Northwest's only retreat center dedicated to providing life-giving retreats, without charge, for people with cancer and for their caregivers. Originally created as a wellness center, Harmony Hill's cancer retreat program was inspired by the internationally acclaimed Commonweal Institute Cancer Help Program in California. In 1994, after viewing Bill Moyers' PBS documentary, "Healing and the Mind," I was fortunate to participate in Commonweal's first training for other centers.

Over the years, Harmony Hill's cancer program has expanded and developed to promote stress reduction; self-care; and physical, emotional, and spiritual well-being. Retreats include nutritional education and delicious homemade meals, yoga, meditation, art projects, and group support. Participants learn how to recover their quality of life despite their physical condition and diagnosis.

Today, Harmony Hill strives to reach any and all whose lives have been touched by cancer, including underserved populations such as African Americans, sexual minorities, and Native Americans. Since 2004, Harmony Hill has offered its remarkable cancer programs free of charge to all who need them. If you feel you might benefit from such an experience, please see page 218 for more information.

The flagship Cancer Program is only part of the Harmony Hill story. Rooted in its inception as a wellness center, Harmony Hill continues to offer moderately priced renewal retreats for health professionals, labyrinth workshops, workshops on guided imagery, cooking healthy comfort foods, yoga for the immune system, and more. These programs, and group rentals of our retreat facilities, provide important financial support for our cancer retreat programs. We are deeply grateful to the several thousand people who participate in them each year.

The kitchen at Harmony Hill remains the heart of this healing home. I hope that as you try these recipes and enjoy our delicious meals, you will experience some of the comfort, serenity, and peace that permeates Harmony Hill.

Gretchen Schodde, ARNP, MN

Executive Director
Harmony Hill, July 2008

Welcome to Harmony Hill

Perched high on a hillside overlooking Washington State's Cascade Mountains and the sparkling waters of Hood Canal, Harmony Hill Retreat Center has been providing cancer retreats for more than 15 years. Our core mission is to transform the experience of cancer through free programs that serve both those with cancer and their caregivers. We also welcome thousands of visitors who attend conferences, meetings, classes, and retreats at the Hill. No matter what brings them here, visitors leave refreshed, relaxed, and very well fed.

Well-organized and hospitable, Harmony Hill's sunny kitchen is a joyful place. We believe that cooking with loving intention is healing in itself, for all concerned. We offer all our guests a lively variety of delicious, seasonal whole foods, many of them homegrown in our organic gardens. Our recipes are influenced by cuisines from around the world. While our menus stress colorful plant-based foods, packed with cancer-fighting phytonutrients and antioxidants, we also serve fish from local waters and organic dairy products.

Because we happily accommodate those who cannot tolerate wheat, eggs, or other common foods, many of our recipes are easily adapted for special dietary needs. Substitutions, additions, and subtractions are noted when appropriate, with suggestions for vegetarians and vegans.

Nutritional tips and kitchen techniques are found throughout the book, which is broadly organized by category and more specifically by season. You may notice a certain amount of overlap from chapter to chapter, since our flavorful dressings and seasonal sauces are linked with appropriate recipes rather than segregated into their own chapter.

The final chapter, "Comfort Food," reflects our rich experience over many years of providing soothing food and a comforting physical and spiritual environment for thousands of guests. Whether you or a loved one is experiencing the cancer journey or not, we hope Harmony Hill's recipes will bring new life to your kitchen. To your health!

Ann Lovejoy
Harmony Hill, July 2008

Cooking at Harmony Hill
Recipes for Hope and Healing

1 Snacks and Appetizers

At Harmony Hill, bowls of fresh fruit and crunchy mixtures of toasted nuts and tiny Japanese snacking crackers are offered at every gathering. Healthy, delicious snacks give active folks an energetic boost between meals, while tempting those with poor appetites to eat a tiny snack every few hours. To be sure this adds up to an adequate diet through the day, serve a little protein with each snack and avoid nonfat foods (unless ordered by your doctor).

If you eat an early breakfast, a midmorning treat of almonds, apple slices, and string cheese will tide you over until lunch. When you get the late afternoon blahs, protein-rich spiced pumpkin seeds, smoked salmon, or a hard-boiled egg deviled with hummus make terrific pick-me-ups. If you are a bedtime snacker, a mug of hot milk with real vanilla and fresh nutmeg will help you sleep.

Healthy snacks combine lean protein with beneficial fats and less-dense carbohydrates. Try spreading whole grain pita breads or crispbread with hummus, ricotta, or goat cheese, then add olives, fresh vegetables, and chopped herbs for extra flavor. Use crisp Romaine lettuce leaves instead of crackers, and include fruit or vegetables in every snack. This chapter contains many more ideas for fast, nutritious, and tasty snacks.

Savory Snack Platter
Spicy Pumpkin Seeds
Tasty Tidbits
Herbed Salmon Spread
Hummus
Hummus Deviled Eggs
Easy Toasted Nuts
Rainbow Vegetable Plate with
    Cilantro Dressing
Cilantro Dressing

Thai Fresh Spring Rolls
    (Gluten-Free)
Almond Butter
Seed and Nut Celery Sticks
Harmony Hill Spiced Nut Mix
Harmony Hill Summer Salsa
Summer Stripes
Brine-Cured Olive Tapenade
Goat Cheese with Fresh Herbs
Stuffed Mushrooms

What retreat participants say about Harmony Hill:

"Everything is exceptional. The graceful, generous, thoughtful staff and service. The unbelievably perfect and nurturing food, so richly and delicately prepared. The caring and pure energy of the land—labyrinths, garden, water, the cottages and the character enfolded in them. I appreciate the close attention to sustainability."

"This is THE most peaceful place I have been."

"Each trip to Harmony Hill has been a truly serendipitous journey to personal health."

"I came back to myself here."

"The food nourished body and spirit with beauty and substance. The retreat provided a professional, warm, and hospitable environment to explore and gain skills and to find new hope in the journey with cancer."

Savory Snack Platter

For seasonal variety, use crisp steamed vegetables such as asparagus, green beans, or slim spears of Romanesco broccoli.

    12 small leaves Romaine lettuce
    4 ounces feta cheese, crumbled
    4 ounces smoked tuna or salmon, sliced
    2 hard-boiled eggs, sliced
    1 cup cherry tomatoes, halved
    1 cup cucumber, thinly sliced
    1/4 cup Niçoise olives, pitted
    1/4 cup basil, shredded

Arrange ingredients on a platter and serve (use lettuce as you would crackers and top with desired ingredients). Serves 4.

Spicy Pumpkin Seeds

High in protein and low in carbohydrates, pumpkin seeds make a terrific on-the-go snack.

    3 cups raw hulled pumpkin seeds
    1 tablespoon virgin olive oil
    1 tablespoon Chipotle Tabasco® Sauce
    1/4 teaspoon lemon pepper seasoning or
        1/4 teaspoon curry powder

Preheat oven to 300 degrees F. Gently toss pumpkin seeds with remaining ingredients and spread one layer deep on a rimmed baking sheet. Bake until toasted (8–10 minutes). Makes 12 snack servings.

"Wow, can I eat here every day?!?"

Tasty Tidbits

In season, combine pear slices with blue cheese, peaches with Pepper Jack, or tangerines with extra sharp cheddar.

> 1 Pink Lady or any tart apple, cut in 12 slices
> 12 leaves fresh basil
> 2 ounces feta or fresh goat cheese, crumbled
> 24 toasted almonds

Wrap each apple slice in a basil leaf with cheese and almonds. Divide between two plates and serve. Serves 2.

Herbed Salmon Spread

This delectable spread is a splendid way to use up leftover grilled or poached salmon. Smooth, creamy quark is a fresh farmer's cheese that packs a lot of protein. To make a lactose-free version, substitute plain soft tofu for the cheese and add a teaspoon of lemon juice.

> 1/2 cup quark or cottage cheese (nonfat works fine)
> 1 tablespoon Dijon-style mustard
> 1 tablespoon Italian parsley, minced
> 2 teaspoons fresh chives, minced
> 1 teaspoon fresh dill, minced
> 1/4 teaspoon Bragg Liquid Aminos or sea salt
> 1 cup cooked salmon, flaked

In a food processor, combine all ingredients and puree until smooth (1–2 minutes). Serve immediately with apple slices and crackers or chill overnight. Makes about 1 1/2 cups.

Tip Bragg Liquid Aminos is a soy-derived protein concentrate that contains 16 amino acids, making it a valuable supplement for vegans and vegetarians. Bragg adds the rich, savory quality called "umame" to plant-based foods. Gluten-free and neither heated nor fermented, Bragg makes an excellent lower-salt replacement for soy sauce.

Hummus

A Harmony Hill favorite, this delicious dip gets extra protein from tofu—a secret ingredient nobody ever guesses. Serve hummus with raw vegetables or spread on a crusty baguette.

2 1/2 cups cooked garbanzo beans, drained
1/3 cup tahini
3 cloves garlic, chopped
1 teaspoon kosher or sea salt
1/2 teaspoon freshly ground black pepper
1 pound plain firm tofu, drained and chopped
2–3 organic lemons, juiced, rind grated
    or 1/3 cup lemon juice
1/3 cup hulled raw sesame seeds
2 teaspoons ground cumin
3 green onions, finely chopped
2 tablespoons minced green onion tops

In a food processor, puree garbanzos, tahini, garlic, salt, and pepper (mixture will be thick). Add tofu, lemon rind (if using), and 1/2 cup juice and puree until creamy. In a wide, shallow pan over medium high heat, dry toast sesame seeds until they pop (2–3 minutes). Cook, stirring, until lightly browned (2–3 minutes). Add 2 tablespoons toasted seeds to bean mixture and set remainder aside. Toast cumin in the pan until fragrant (about 1 minute) and add to beans with chopped onions. Pulse to blend, stir in remaining seeds and minced onion tips and serve. Refrigerate for up to a week. Makes about 3 1/2 cups.

"Beautiful surroundings, incredible gardens, fantastic and fresh and healthful meals, but most of all, the loving and caregiving staff, who strive to make us comfortable at all times."

Cooking at Harmony Hill

Hummus Deviled Eggs

An enticing variation on our favorite finger food!

    4 hard-boiled eggs, halved
    1/4 cup plain or spicy hummus
    1/4 teaspoon smoked paprika

In a bowl, mash egg yolks with hummus. Stuff eggs and serve, garnished with paprika. Serves 4.

Easy Toasted Nuts

Nutritious, delicious, and easy to tuck in your purse, toasted nuts are an excellent snack. To keep added oils and salt at a minimum, toast your own.

1 cup raw almonds	15–20 minutes
1 cup raw hazelnuts	15–20 minutes
1 cup raw cashews	10–12 minutes
1 cup raw walnut halves	10–12 minutes
1 cup raw peanuts	10–12 minutes

Preheat oven to 350 degrees F. Arrange nuts in a single layer on a rimmed baking sheet and bake until crisp. (See chart above for suggested times.) Cool and store in a closed container for up to 2 weeks.

"The staff provides a loving atmosphere where healing and acceptance may begin. I wish all individuals could experience the support that Harmony Hill offers."

Rainbow Vegetable Plate with Cilantro Dressing

Serve this beautiful dish at your next family gathering and watch these wholesome goodies disappear. To your health!

    1 cup purple cauliflower, cut in florets
    1 cup orange cauliflower, cut in florets
    1 cup Romanesco broccoli, cut in florets
    1 cup broccoflower, cut in florets
    1 Purple Haze or Rainbow carrot, cut in 1-inch pieces
    1 each red, yellow, white, and orange carrots,
        cut in 1-inch pieces
    1 cup Cilantro Dressing (see below)

Arrange vegetables on a platter with Cilantro Dressing in the middle. Serves 6–8.

Cilantro Dressing

    1 cup cilantro, stemmed
    2 cloves garlic, chopped
    1/2 cup olive oil
    1/4 cup brown rice vinegar
    1/4 teaspoon kosher or sea salt
    1/4 teaspoon freshly ground black pepper

In a blender, puree all ingredients. Makes about 1 1/2 cups dressing. Refrigerate leftovers for up to 2 days.

Thai Fresh Spring Rolls (Gluten-Free)

Found in the Asian food section of large grocery stores, thin discs of tapioca flour make soft wraps for all sorts of savory or sweet treats. These gluten-free tapioca spring roll wrappers are also delicious with ricotta and blueberries or strawberries.

12 tapioca spring roll wrappers
4–6 ounces cooked, cleaned shrimp
4 green onions, thinly sliced
1 cup daikon radish sprouts or bean sprouts,
    rinsed and patted dry
1/2 cup finely grated or shredded carrot
1 tablespoon fresh mint, minced
1/4 cup Thai sweet red chilli sauce

If using dried tapioca sheets, fill a wide, shallow bowl with water and add the sheets one at a time.

Combine remaining ingredients and assemble spring rolls as follows. Remove a wrap from the water and place it on a plate. Add about 2 tablespoons of filling, then fold over the top and bottom and roll up the sides. Place each wrap on a serving platter (do not overlap). Let sit until translucent (about 5 minutes), then serve. Makes 12 spring rolls.

Almond Butter

Expensive to buy and hard to find without additives, fresh nut butters are a simple luxury. If you keep toasted nuts on hand, you can whip up a batch in about 3 minutes.

1 1/2 cup raw almonds (or any nut)
1/8 teaspoon kosher or sea salt
2–3 teaspoons canola or almond oil

Preheat oven to 350 degrees F. Place nuts in a single layer on a rimmed baking sheet and bake at 350 to desired crispness (15–20 minutes). In a food processor, grind toasted nuts to desired consistency for smooth or crunchy nut butter. Add salt and drizzle in oil until mixture clumps. Refrigerate in a tightly sealed glass jar for up to a month. Makes about 1 cup.

"Harmony Hill is a sacred, healing place."

Seed and Nut Celery Sticks

Not just for kids, this pretty, simple, and surprisingly tasty snack is also good with thinly sliced fennel and toasted sunflower seeds.

>   6 stalks celery, ends trimmed
>   1/3 cup almond butter or any nut butter
>   3 tablespoons toasted pumpkin or sesame seeds

Fill each piece of celery with nut butter, gently roll in seeds and serve. Serves 2.

Harmony Hill Spiced Nut Mix

An ounce or so a day of nuts offers protection against heart disease and reduces the risk of developing diabetes. Here's a festive way to enjoy them.

>   2 tablespoons virgin olive oil
>   1 tablespoon Worcestershire Sauce
>   1 tablespoon Chipotle Tabasco® Sauce
>   1 cup almonds
>   1 cup hazelnuts
>   1 cup walnuts
>   1 teaspoon mild chili powder

Preheat oven to 300 degrees F. Toss oil, sauces, and nuts to coat well, then toss in chili powder and spread one layer deep on a rimmed baking sheet. Bake until toasted (15–20 minutes). Makes 12 snack servings.

"Harmony Hill has been a place of healing with no judgment on who you are, where you are in your journey, and how you deal with cancer. It provides one-of-a-kind support."

Harmony Hill Summer Salsa

Pass this with raw vegetables, baked chips, or thin slices of apple. It's also excellent over mixed greens or couscous.

    1 tablespoon lime juice
    1 clove garlic, minced or pressed
    1/4 cup cilantro, stemmed
    1 tablespoon mint, stemmed and chopped
    1/8 teaspoon salt
    2 cups cherry tomatoes, cut in half
    1 ripe avocado, diced
    1/2 cup red or sweet onion, chopped

Combine all ingredients and let stand for at least 15 minutes. Serve with chips or raw vegetables. Makes about 2 cups.

Summer Stripes

To make this fancy-looking treat savory instead of sweet, replace sugar with 1/4 teaspoon of black pepper.

    2 cups raspberries
    1 teaspoon fresh mint
    2 cups cantaloupe, pureed
    1 tablespoon fresh basil
    1/8 teaspoon sea salt
    2 cups blackberries, pureed
    2 teaspoons sugar

In a food processor, puree raspberries and mint, pour into four 1-cup dishes; freeze until set (about 1 hour). Puree cantaloupe, basil, and salt, pour over raspberry layer; freeze until set (about 1 hour). Repeat with blackberries and sugar; freeze until set. To serve, place each cup in warm water for 2 minutes, then turn out onto a salad plate. Serves 4.

Tip Freeze fresh berry puree in popsicle molds for a refreshing and healthy treat for kids.

Brine-Cured Olive Tapenade

Olives and olive oils provide stable, beneficial, and delicious fats that help us absorb minerals and vitamins. Canned olives are often bland and tasteless (and may be dyed to disguise unripeness). For best flavor, choose brine-cured, tree-ripened black olives such as Kalamata, Gaeta, or Niçoise. For a brighter flavor, add grated organic lemon peel and a teaspoon of fresh lemon juice.

> 1 cup Kalamata olives, pitted and coarsely chopped
> 1 cup Niçoise olives, pitted and coarsely chopped
> 2 tablespoons capers, drained
> 2 cloves garlic, minced
> 2 tablespoons Italian parsley, minced
> 1/4 teaspoon freshly ground black pepper
> 2 tablespoons virgin olive oil

In a food processor, coarsely puree the olives, capers, garlic, parsley, and pepper. Add the olive oil and puree to desired consistency. Refrigerate for up to a week. Makes about 2 cups.

Goat Cheese with Fresh Herbs

Nutritious, flavorful, and easily digested by the lactose-intolerant, fresh goat cheese has about half the fat and nearly twice the protein of cream cheese. Serve this spread with thin wafers or nut-based crackers for a little more protein.

> 3–4 ounces fresh goat cheese
> 1 tablespoon fresh basil, minced
> 1 tablespoon fresh Italian parsley, minced
> 1/4 teaspoon freshly ground black pepper
> 1/4 teaspoon kosher or sea salt

Blend all ingredients and chill for an hour or overnight. Serve with raw vegetables or crackers. Makes about 1/2 cup.

Stuffed Mushrooms

Plain white mushrooms are not the tastiest, but recent studies show they can markedly enhance immune systems. Brown Crimini mushrooms, baby versions of flavorful Portobellos, taste especially good in this recipe.

12 2-inch mushrooms, brown or white
1 teaspoon virgin olive oil
2 cloves garlic, chopped
1/4 cup pine nuts
1/2 cup feta, crumbled

Preheat oven to 350 degrees F. Stem mushrooms and chop stems, set aside. Gently brush tops clean and place cup side up in a baking dish. In a heavy frying pan, heat oil, garlic, and pine nuts over medium high heat until barely golden (1–2 minutes). Add mushroom stems and cook, covered, for 3 minutes. Stuff mushroom caps, top with feta and bake until hot through (20–30 minutes). Makes 12.

"Retreating at Harmony Hill is like returning to the open arms of the good mother. The location and natural beauty are sensual delights. The warmth and love is palpable. What's not to like? Whole foods cooked with heartfelt passion, which comes through in presentation, versatility, and amazing taste experiences. It became a great part of the soul nurture with nurturing the body. My needs were more than met. I feel fulfilled and filled full."

2 Salads Big and Small

The American Cancer Society and a multitude of researchers encourage us to move toward a plant-based diet, while the USDA now recommends up to nine daily servings of vegetables. One great way to enjoy a wide range of vegetables is to serve fresh salads daily. Happily, salads come in almost infinite variety, with delightful options for every season.

Harmony Hill meals often feature several salads, some with leafy greens and others rich with vegetables. Fruit, both fresh and dried, makes a frequent appearance in salads as well as in our savory dressings. In this chapter, you'll find an inspiring assortment of delectable entrée and side salads, with suggestions for seasonal or dietary tweaking.

The dressings alone provide a treasure trove of flavor sparks to turn a simple green salad into a palate-pleasing treat. Try them with grilled fish or chicken as well as over steamed vegetables, and feel free to exchange your favorite herbs, fruits, and spices for our choices.

The greatest nutritional benefit comes from the brightest leafy greens and the most richly colored fruits and vegetables. Recent research shows that the more colorful an edible plant, the higher it is in cancer-fighting phytonutrients. To get full benefit from the plant pantry, push past the usual supermarket fare. Visit farmer's markets or grow your own colorful Rainbow carrots, Easter Egg radishes, pink and blue potatoes, and golden or purple cauliflower, all of which taste as good as they look.

WINTER

Rainbow Salad with
  Pear Dressing
Pear Dressing
Beet and Orange Salad
Winter Wonderland Salad
Curried Carrot Salad
Harmony Hill Super Slaw
Fresh Apple Dressing
Winter Green Pasta Salad

SPRING

Spunky Spring Greens
Spring Herb Dressing
Fennel Salad with Hot
  Asparagus Dressing
Hot Asparagus Dressing
Easter Egg Radish Salad
Strawberry Salad
Fresh Strawberry Dressing
Fusilli with Fresh Peas and Feta
Creamy Tuscan Dressing

SUMMER

Peachy Green Salad with
  Blackberry Dressing
Blackberry Dressing
Spicy Melon Salad
Black Bean Salad with
  Tomatillo Salsa
Tomatillo Salsa
Blueberry Salad
Blueberry Lime Dressing
Curried Corn Salad
Curry Dressing
Deviled Egg Salad with Basil
  Pesto Dressing
Basil Pesto Dressing
Italian Hot Potato Salad

FALL

Sunset Salad
Mango Chutney Dressing
Harmony Hill Waldorf Salad
Festive Fall Salad
Italian White Bean Salad
  with Tuna
Caper Dressing
Pepper Pear Salad
White Knight Salad
Hot Onion Dressing

"The retreat far exceeded any expectations I had. I've gained new coping skills that will become part of me. The retreat provides a safe place to talk about things that make other people (in other settings) very uncomfortable."

Rainbow Salad
with Pear Dressing

The Rainbow Diet encourages us to eat food from every color group every day. The cabbage family offers some of nature's most powerful cancer fighters in shades of red, white, green, and purple. Supplement freely with your favorite vegetables.

>   1 cup Tuscan kale or red chard, finely sliced
>   1 cup Savoy cabbage, shredded
>   1 cup Napa cabbage, shredded
>   1 cup red cabbage, shredded
>   1 yellow bell pepper, thinly sliced
>   1 carrot, grated
>   1 cup purple broccoli, cut in florets
>   1/2 ripe pear, cored, peeled, and diced
>   1/4 cup Italian parsley, chopped
>   1 cup Pear Dressing (see below)

Combine greens and arrange on four plates. Top with vegetables and pear and serve with Pear Dressing. Serves 4.

Pear Dressing

Try this with cumin or celery seed instead of fennel seed, and serve it with grilled fish or roast chicken.

>   1 ripe pear, cored, peeled, and mashed
>   1 clove garlic, minced or pressed
>   1 teaspoon fennel seed
>   1/4 cup virgin olive oil
>   1–2 tablespoons cider vinegar
>   1/4 teaspoon kosher or sea salt
>   1/4 teaspoon freshly ground black pepper

In a food processor, combine all ingredients and puree for 10 seconds. Refrigerate for up to 2 days. Makes about 1 cup.

Beet and Orange Salad

Most flavorful served at room temperature, this refreshing salad is a lovely way to use up cooked beets. If you use canned beets, choose brands that contain just beets and salt.

    1 organic orange, rind grated
    2 cups (1 15-ounce can) julienned beets, drained
    1/4 cup red onion, finely chopped
    1/4 teaspoon sea salt
    1/4 teaspoon freshly ground black pepper
    few grains freshly ground nutmeg (optional)
    1–2 teaspoons fresh lime or lemon juice

Slice white pith off orange, section and chop fruit and place in a bowl with grated rind. Add drained beets, onion, salt and pepper, and nutmeg (if using) and season to taste with lime or lemon juice. Makes about 2 cups. Chill or serve immediately. Serves 4–6.

Variation For Orange Jicama Salad, proceed as above, substituting 2 cups julienned jicama for the beets.

Tip Slicing off orange pith is far faster than peeling, and orange chunks look just as pretty as hand-peeled pieces.

"Food? Fab! Creative. Flavorful. Made with l-o-v-e."

"This place is wonderful! Calming, tranquil. The labyrinths and the food are unique! Fabulous!"

"The most delicious food I've ever had."

Winter Wonderland Salad

Excellent with grilled fish or roasted chicken, this all-white melange is also wonderful over cooked oat groats or quinoa.

    2 tablespoons unsweetened, shredded coconut
    1 Braeburn or Honeycrisp apple, cored and diced
    1 Bosc or Bartlett pear, cored and diced
    1 ripe banana, thinly sliced
    1/2 cup fennel, thinly sliced
    1/4 teaspoon cinnamon
    2–3 teaspoons lime juice

Bake coconut on a baking sheet at 350 degrees F until lightly golden (8–10 minutes). Set aside. In a bowl, combine apple, pear, banana, fennel, cinnamon, and lime juice. Toss gently to coat and serve, sprinkled with toasted coconut. Serves 4.

Curried Carrot Salad

Quick, delicious, and pretty on the plate, this spicy salad can be made ahead and chilled until serving time. Vivid orange carrots promote eye health and strengthen the immune system, while onions contain potent antioxidants.

    1 cup plain yogurt or sour cream (nonfat works fine)
    1 teaspoon garam masala or curry powder
    2 cups grated carrots
    1/4 cup red onion, chopped
    2 tablespoons golden raisins
    2 teaspoons fresh lime juice

In a bowl, combine yogurt and garam masala, set aside. Toss carrots, red onion, and raisins with lime juice, then stir in yogurt and serve. Makes about 2 cups. Serves 4.

Variation Make a dairy-free version by replacing the yogurt with soft tofu (process in blender to make a smoother sauce).

Harmony Hill Super Slaw

One of our most popular salads. For variety, try replacing cilantro with balsamic vinegar and pine nuts, or half a teaspoon of curry powder and toasted peanuts, or a blend of cumin and fennel seed.

    1 cup green cabbage, shredded
    1 cup red cabbage, shredded
    1 carrot, grated
    2 stalks celery, grated
    1 Gala or Fuji apple, cored and grated
    1/4 cup cilantro or parsley, stemmed
    1/2 cup Fresh Apple Dressing (see below)

In a serving bowl, toss cabbage, carrot, celery, apple, and cilantro with dressing. Chill or serve immediately. Makes about 3 cups. Serves 4–6.

Fresh Apple Dressing

    1/4 cup cider vinegar
    1/4 cup apple, finely chopped
    1 tablespoon mayonnaise (lowfat works fine)
    1 shallot or garlic clove, minced or pressed
    2 teaspoons Grade B maple syrup or sugar
    1/4 teaspoon Bragg Liquid Aminos or soy sauce
    1/4 teaspoon smoked paprika

Combine all ingredients and shake to blend. Refrigerate leftovers for up to 2 days. Makes about 1/2 cup.

"I am so thankful and grateful that these programs exist for groups like us. This is truly unique, an experience like no other. The staff here are absolutely amazing, wonderful, and caring people. Please continue these programs—they transform one's soul in such a positive way. Thank you."

Winter Green Pasta Salad

This satisfying pasta salad tastes great when served hot and mellows pleasantly when chilled. The pureed tomato dressing tastes amazingly fresh at any time of year.

    1 15-ounce can or 1 1/2 cups diced tomatoes with juice
    8–10 ounces dried rotini or any pasta
    1 tablespoon virgin olive oil
    2 shallots or garlic cloves, thinly sliced
    1 white or yellow onion, chopped
    1/4 teaspoon kosher or sea salt
    1/2 teaspoon smoked paprika
    2 cups Black Tuscan kale, shredded
    6 cups young spinach
    2 tablespoons flat Italian parsley, stemmed
    1–2 ounces hard cheese such as Romano or Pecorino,
        in wide shavings (use a vegetable peeler)

In a food processor or blender, puree half the tomatoes with juice for 10 seconds, set aside. Cook pasta according to package directions. While water is heating, heat oil and shallots or garlic, onions, salt, and paprika in a wide, shallow pan over medium high heat for 3 minutes. Add kale and spinach, cover pan and cook until lightly wilted (3–4 minutes). Add remaining tomatoes, cover pan and remove from heat. In a large bowl, toss hot, drained pasta with greens mixture, stir in pureed tomatoes and serve, garnished with parsley and cheese. Serves 4–6.

"Surprisingly good food (I am a meat-eater generally). The love that goes into the food preparation must be your secret ingredient. You can taste the love."

Spunky Spring Greens

If you like dandelion greens, this is a great way to use them.

2 cups mixed young salad greens
1 cup baby kale, shredded
2 cups baby spinach, stemmed
2 cups Napa cabbage, thinly sliced
1/4 cup flat Italian parsley, stemmed
2 tablespoons fresh sorrel, shredded
1 tablespoon fresh lemon balm, shredded
Spring Herb Dressing (see below)

Combine all greens in a serving bowl, dress lightly, toss and serve. Serves 4–6.

Spring Herb Dressing

1/2 cup virgin olive oil
1/3 cup brown rice vinegar
1/2 teaspoon fresh thyme, stemmed
1 teaspoon fresh fennel greens, shredded
1 teaspoon fresh garlic tips or chives, chopped
1 tablespoon fresh parsley, stemmed and chopped
1 tablespoon French sorrel, shredded
1/8 teaspoon salt
1/4 teaspoon freshly ground black pepper

In a food processor, combine all ingredients and process for 10 seconds. Serve over tossed greens or steamed vegetables. Refrigerate any leftovers. Makes about 1 cup.

"The food was better than in a five-star restaurant. All facilities are exceptionally clean and lovingly decorated. I came here exhausted after working all day and I'm leaving with love and peace in my heart, more courage to meet 'bad' days when they come. I made lots of new friends. "

Fennel Salad with Hot Asparagus Dressing

A wonderful way to appreciate the first local asparagus.

    4 cups baby spinach
    2 cups mixed red and green baby Romaine lettuce
    1 cup bok choy, shredded
    1 bulb fennel, finely chopped (including greens)
    Hot Asparagus Dressing (see below)
    4 green onions, finely sliced

Gently toss greens and fennel. Divide among four dinner plates. Top with dressing and serve, garnished with green onions. Serves 4.

Hot Asparagus Dressing

Fast and spunky, this hot dressing is also fabulous spooned over boiled new potatoes, grilled fish, or baked chicken.

    1 teaspoon virgin olive oil
    2 cloves garlic, chopped
    1/4 cup onion, chopped
    1/4 teaspoon sea salt
    1 teaspoon capers, drained
    12 spears asparagus, ends trimmed, chopped

In a wide, shallow pan, heat oil and garlic over medium high heat for 2 minutes. Add onion, salt, and capers and cook for 2 minutes. Add asparagus, cover pan and cook until bright green and barely tender (2–3 minutes). Spoon over greens and serve. Serves 4.

"Everyone we encountered and interacted with was kind, generous, and filled with love. The beauty of this place astounds me."

Easter Egg Radish Salad

Easter Egg radishes come in shades of rose, red, purple, and cream, making a delicious and beautiful garnish. Colorful Rainbow carrots combine a varied mixture of phytonutrients with sweet crunchiness.

    1 cup yogurt or sour cream (lowfat works fine)
    1 tablespoon shallot, minced
    1 tablespoon chives, minced
    1/4 teaspoon shoyu or soy sauce
    1/4 cup golden raisins
    1/2 cup celery, thinly chopped
    1/2 cup Easter Egg radishes, thinly sliced
    1 cup Rainbow carrots, thinly sliced

For the dressing, combine yogurt, shallot, chives, and soy sauce and let stand for at least 15 minutes. In a serving bowl, combine raisins, celery, half the radishes, and carrots. Toss with dressing and serve, garnished with remaining radish slices. Serves 4.

"I learned about the Center from a dear friend whose life was transformed by her retreat there. Before she went, she was bitter, frightened, and angry about her diagnosis. But after she returned, she was the most intensely alive person I have ever known, despite the fact that hers was a fairly rapidly terminal disease. I recently assisted at a retreat as a housekeeper and saw the power of this process to help those with this disease reconnect to their inner strength and joy, and leave, still with cancer, but more peaceful, alive, and committed to living life to its fullest every day. I felt transformed just by watching."

Strawberry Salad

The first fruit of spring tastes delightfully complex in this peppery salad. It's also lovely with raspberries or loganberries later in the summer.

    8 leaves of butter or Boston lettuce
    1/4 red onion, thinly sliced
    12 fresh strawberries, sliced and fanned
    1 teaspoon capers, drained
    2–3 ounces fresh goat cheese
    Fresh Strawberry Dressing (see below)

On four salad plates, arrange lettuce and top with red onion. Fan berries on each plate and top with capers and goat cheese. Drizzle with dressing and serve. Serves 4.

Fresh Strawberry Dressing

Try this with black raspberries or Marionberries, and toss with mixed greens or a fruity salad.

    1/4 cup strawberries, chopped
    1/3 cup canola or safflower oil
    2 tablespoons white balsamic or cider vinegar
    1/4 teaspoon freshly ground black pepper
    1/8 teaspoon sea salt

In a food processor, combine all ingredients and puree until smooth. Makes about 2/3 cup.

"The group discussions were the most valuable to me. The encouragement to open up and share helped me establish some inner peace with my cancer."

Fusilli with Fresh Peas and Feta

Made in minutes, this pretty salad can be a main dish at lunch or served with soup and a warm roll in the evening.

2 cups fusilli or bowtie pasta
1 cup snow peas in pods, ends trimmed
1 carrot, grated
1 red or yellow bell pepper, sliced
1 cup Creamy Tuscan Dressing (see below)
4 ounces feta cheese, crumbled

Cook pasta according to package directions. While water is heating, toss together the peas, carrot, and pepper. Toss with hot, drained pasta and Creamy Tuscan Dressing and garnish with feta. Serves 4.

Creamy Tuscan Dressing

Fresh rosemary gives this almost instant sauce an Italian flair, but it's also delicious with basil, fennel, or thyme.

1 cup yogurt, quark, or sour cream (nonfat works fine)
2 cloves garlic, chopped
1 tablespoon lemon juice
1 teaspoon rosemary, stemmed and chopped
1/4 teaspoon kosher or sea salt
1/4 teaspoon freshly ground black pepper

In a food processor or blender, combine all ingredients and puree. Refrigerate for up to 3 days. Makes about 1 cup.

Variation For a vegan version, use soft tofu instead of yogurt.

"Healing, harmonious atmosphere: so very close to nature; a place of miracles; wholesome, natural, delicious food; safe place; friendly, helpful staff."

Peachy Green Salad
with Blackberry Dressing

To keep this luscious salad evenly distributed, assemble it
directly on the plates.

    4 cups young mixed greens
    1 cup fresh spinach, stemmed and shredded
    1 cup green cabbage, finely shredded
    1 cup cucumber, thinly sliced
    1/2 Walla Walla Sweet onion, finely diced
    2 ripe peaches or nectarines, diced
    2 stalks celery, finely sliced
    1/4 cup cilantro, stemmed
    Blackberry Dressing (see below)
    1/4 cup toasted almonds, chopped

In a large bowl, toss greens, spinach, and cabbage. In a small
bowl, gently toss cucumber, onion, peaches, celery, and cilantro.
Divide greens among four dinner plates and top with peach
mixture. Drizzle with dressing and garnish with nuts. Serves 4.

Blackberry Dressing

Spicy and fragrant, this lovely dressing is also loaded with
antioxidants and phytonutrients.

    1 cup fresh blackberries
    1 teaspoon sugar, maple syrup, or honey
    1 shallot or garlic clove, minced or pressed
    1/2 teaspoon coriander or cumin
    1/8 teaspoon salt
    1/8 teaspoon freshly ground black or white pepper
    1/4 cup virgin olive oil
    1 tablespoon balsamic vinegar

Combine all ingredients in a food processor and puree to blend.
Makes about 1 1/3 cups. Refrigerate leftovers for up to 2 days.

Spicy Melon Salad

Piquant and pleasing, this unusual salad provides a lively contrast to grilled fish or chicken.

    1 tablespoon sweet red Thai chilli sauce
    1/2 cup Walla Walla Sweet onion
    2 cups melon, peeled, seeded, and diced
    2 cups watermelon, peeled and diced
    2 cups cantaloupe, peeled, seeded, and diced
    1/4 cup cilantro, stemmed

Combine all ingredients and let stand for 15 minutes. Serves 4–6.

"Not only was the cuisine of very high quality, fresh, and nourishing, but it always gave me the feeling that it had been prepared and charged up with love, more a work of art than mere food for our bodies. Breathtaking, inspiring."

"How do I begin to find words to say how beautiful and special the staff are? They made me feel special, and at home, more at home than I do in my own home, if that makes any sense!"

"I'm inspired to find a way to give back."

Black Bean Salad
with Tomatillo Salsa

This simple salad offers surprisingly complex flavors, especially when drizzled with zesty Tomatillo Salsa.

    2 cups cooked black beans, drained
    1/4 cup red or sweet onion, chopped
    1 cup cucumber, chopped
    1 cup cilantro, stemmed
    1 teaspoon cumin
    1/2 teaspoon chipotle Tabasco® sauce
    1 cup Tomatillo Salsa (see below)

Combine all ingredients and let stand for at least an hour or refrigerate overnight. Serves 4.

Tomatillo Salsa

This tart, tangy tomatillo salsa tastes great with Yellow Pear tomatoes, but it's lovely with any tart-sweet cherry tomato. Enjoy it with chips or raw vegetables or over fish or chicken.

    2 teaspoons virgin olive oil
    1 Ancho or Jalapeno chile, seeded and finely chopped
    1 sweet red pepper, chopped
    2 cloves garlic, chopped
    1 cup tomatillos, husked and chopped
    2 cups Yellow Pear or any cherry tomatoes, cut in half
    1 cup cantaloupe or any melon, diced
    1/2 cup red or sweet onion, finely chopped
    1/4 cup cilantro, stemmed
    2 tablespoons cider vinegar

In a heavy frying pan, heat oil, chile pepper, sweet pepper, and garlic over medium high heat. Cook, stirring, until garlic is pale golden (2–3 minutes), then add tomatillos and cook, stirring, until barely soft (3–5 minutes). Remove from pan and combine with remaining ingredients, adding vinegar to taste (start with 1 tablespoon). Makes about 3 cups. Refrigerate for up to 3 days.

Cooking at Harmony Hill

Note Always wear gloves when handling chile peppers. If you do get "chile burn," any over-the-counter antihistamine will quickly chill the flames.

Blueberry Salad

Blueberries offer more antioxidants than any other garden fruit. Their complex, subtle flavor lends itself to both sweet and savory dishes like this one.

2 cups spinach, stemmed
2 cups Romaine or head lettuce, shredded
1 cup blueberries, stemmed
1 cucumber, peeled, seeded, and chopped
Blueberry Lime Dressing (see below)

In a large bowl, combine all ingredients, toss gently and serve. Serves 4.

Blueberry Lime Dressing

Try this luscious, spicy dressing with fruit salad, steamed vegetables, mixed greens, or grilled fish.

1/2 cup olive or canola oil
1 cup blueberries, stemmed
1 clove garlic, chopped
1 organic lime, juiced, rind grated
1 tablespoon balsamic vinegar
1 tablespoon mint, minced
1/8 teaspoon kosher salt

In a food processor, combine all ingredients and puree for 10 seconds or to desired consistency. Makes about 1 cup. Refrigerate leftovers for up to 3 days.

"A safe spot in the universe where I felt instantly at home."

Curried Corn Salad

This savory salad is one of Harmony Hill's most-requested recipes. Try this with super sweet bicolor corn for a real treat.

   1/4 cup green onions, sliced
   1/4 cup celery, chopped
   1/4 cup sweet pepper (red, orange, or yellow)
   1 cup ripe tomato, diced
   4 ears sweet corn, kernels cut from cob
   Curry Dressing (see below)

Combine onion, celery, pepper, tomato, and corn and let stand for at least 15 minutes. Add dressing, toss gently and serve. Makes about 6 cups.

Curry Dressing

Lightly spicy, this simple dressing is also terrific with green beans, summer squash, or tomatoes.

   3 tablespoons canola oil
   1/3 cup rice vinegar
   1 tablespoon sweet or mild curry powder
   1/2 teaspoon salt or Bragg Liquid Aminos or soy sauce

Combine all ingredients and serve over vegetables or greens. Makes about 1/2 cup.

"Food was tremendously refreshing and restoring. I feel so fortunate to have been gifted this experience and wish it for all cancer survivors...a miraculous, special place."

Deviled Egg Salad with Basil Pesto Dressing

Deviled eggs always vanish first at picnics and potlucks. Here's a wholesome, delicious salad that gets gobbled up just as fast.

6 cups mixed greens
1 red sweet pepper, thinly sliced
1/4 cup sweet onion, finely chopped
4 eggs, hard-boiled and cut in half lengthwise
1 cup Basil Pesto Dressing (see below)
1 tablespoon capers, drained

In a bowl, combine greens, red pepper, and onion. Scoop egg yolks into a bowl and blend with 1/3 cup of Basil Pesto Dressing. Refill egg whites with yolk mixture. Gently toss greens with remaining pesto dressing and arrange on four dinner plates, top each with eggs and serve, garnished with capers. Serves 4.

Tip For easy peeling, boil eggs that are at least 4 days old.

Basil Pesto Dressing

Serve this over sliced tomatoes, mixed greens, baked potatoes, or steamed green beans.

1 cup basil, stemmed and shredded
1 cup sour cream (nonfat works fine)
2 cloves garlic, chopped
1 organic lemon, juiced, rind grated
1/4 teaspoon freshly ground black pepper
1/4 teaspoon kosher or sea salt

In a blender or food processor, combine basil, sour cream, garlic, lemon juice and rind, pepper, and salt. Process to a smooth paste. Makes about 1 cup.

Italian Hot Potato Salad

Cooking the potatoes with garlic, just until tender crisp, helps them hold their shape and texture well. For a hearty main dish, use 6 potatoes and add cooked shrimp or hard-boiled eggs.

> 4–6 Yukon Gold potatoes, thinly sliced
> 1/2 teaspoon kosher or sea salt
> 3 cloves garlic, minced or pressed
> 1 tablespoon balsamic or wine vinegar
> 1/4 teaspoon freshly ground pepper
> 1 teaspoon fresh rosemary, stemmed and chopped
> 1 tablespoon virgin olive oil
> 2 stalks celery, sliced
> 1/2 cup red or sweet onion, chopped
> 1 red pepper, finely chopped
> 1/2 cup yogurt or sour cream (nonfat works fine)
> 2 tablespoons mayonnaise
> 1/2 cup fresh basil, shredded
> 1 bunch flat Italian parsley, stemmed (about 2 cups)

In a saucepan, cover potatoes with water. Add 1/4 teaspoon salt and half the garlic, bring to a boil over medium high heat. Reduce heat and simmer until tender (8–10 minutes). Drain and put in a serving bowl. Sprinkle immediately with vinegar, salt, pepper, and rosemary, then drizzle with oil and toss with celery, onion, and sweet pepper. In a food processor, combine remaining garlic, sour cream, mayonnaise, basil, and parsley. Gently toss with potatoes and serve. Serves 4–6.

"Food: fabulous! Hearty and vegetarian is not easy to master, but it's alive and well at Harmony Hill."

"I liked the balance between 'active physical,' 'active emotional,' and 'self' time."

"I came expecting to get very little out of this. I'm overwhelmed with how the experience has enriched my life."

Sunset Salad

Glowing citrus fruit in sunset tones make this savory salad as beautiful as it is delicious. Substitute tangerines, grapefruit, clementines, or pomelos freely.

4–6 cups baby spinach, stemmed
4 cups young greens
1 blood orange, sectioned and chopped
1/2 ruby grapefruit, sectioned and chopped
2 satsumas, sectioned and chopped
4 green onions, thinly sliced
1/4 cup toasted peanuts, chopped
Mango Chutney Dressing (see below)

In a serving bowl, gently toss greens with citrus sections, green onions, and nuts. Chill or serve at once, tossed with Mango Chutney Dressing and garnished with peanuts. Serves 4–6.

Mango Chutney Dressing

What could be easier? You'll be amazed at how complex this dressing tastes.

1/3 cup virgin olive oil
1/3 cup balsamic or cider vinegar
1/4 cup mango chutney, finely chopped

Combine all ingredients in a blender or food processor and puree for 10 seconds. Serve at once or refrigerate for up to a week. Makes about 1 cup.

"The food is unique and exceptional."

Harmony Hill Waldorf Salad

A classic for nearly a century, this is a great way to entice reluctant kids to start enjoying salads.

> 8 leaves Boston or butter lettuce
> 3 tablespoons mayonnaise or yogurt (nonfat works fine)
> 1 organic lemon, juiced, rind grated
> 1/4 teaspoon kosher or sea salt
> 1/4 teaspoon freshly ground black pepper
> 1 Fuji or Braeburn apple, diced
> 2 stalks celery, thinly sliced
> 3 tablespoons golden raisins or dried sour cherries
> 1/4 cup toasted walnut pieces

Arrange lettuce like cups on four salad plates. Combine mayonnaise, lemon rind, 1 tablespoon lemon juice, salt, and pepper. Stir in the apple, celery, raisins, and walnuts and scoop onto lettuce cups. Serves 4.

Festive Fall Salad

Crisp fennel, scrumptious Honeycrisp apples, and tender, sweet-as-candy White Japanese turnips provide a light, sparkling counterpoint to rich holiday fare. If you can't find white turnips, small Purple Top turnips work fine.

> 2 cups (about 6 small) White Japanese turnips,
>   finely chopped
> 2 cups bok choy, finely shredded
> 2 cups (1/2 bulb) Florence fennel, finely chopped
> 2 cups (about 2) Honeycrisp apples, finely diced
> 1/2 cup Italian parsley or cilantro, stemmed
> 1 tablespoon lime juice
> 1 teaspoon ponzu soy sauce or 1/2 teaspoon soy sauce

Toss all ingredients and serve. Serves 8–12.

Italian White Bean Salad with Tuna

This vivid, flavorful Italian entrée salad partners crisp fall vegetables with piquant Caper Dressing and creamy goat cheese. Good with any combination of vegetables.

> 2 cups or 1 can White Northern beans, rinsed and drained
> Caper Dressing (see below)
> 6 cups mixed greens
> 1 teaspoon fresh rosemary, stemmed and minced
> 1/4 cup flat Italian parsley, stemmed
> 2 stalks celery, thinly sliced
> 1 cup Florence fennel, finely chopped
> 1 cup orange or purple cauliflower, in small florets
> 1/4 cup red or sweet onion, chopped
> 2 cups grilled tuna, flaked, or 2 7-ounce cans tuna, drained and flaked
> 1/4 cup goat cheese (feta or fresh), crumbled

Combine beans with dressing, set aside. Combine greens with all remaining ingredients except goat cheese. Strain beans from dressing and add to greens. Drizzle with dressing, toss lightly and serve, garnished with cheese. Serves 4–6.

Caper Dressing

This snappy dressing makes an outstanding marinade or sauce for cooked prawns, grilled tuna, or salmon.

> 1/3 cup fruity olive oil
> 3 tablespoons balsamic vinegar
> 2 cloves garlic, finely chopped
> 1/8 teaspoon kosher or sea salt
> 1 tablespoon capers, drained
> 1/2 teaspoon green peppercorns, drained

Combine all ingredients and shake well to emulsify. Refrigerate leftovers for up to a week. Makes about 2/3 cup.

Pepper Pear Salad

Simple yet surprising, this beautiful fall salad offers intriguing textures and luscious flavors.

1 ripe pear, cored and chopped
1/2 red pepper, thinly sliced
1/4 teaspoon freshly ground black pepper
1/2 cup cilantro or Italian parsley, stemmed
2 tablespoons balsamic vinaigrette
2 cups baby Romaine, torn in half
2 cups Napa cabbage, finely shredded
1 cup red cabbage, finely shredded

In a large bowl, combine pear, red pepper, black pepper, and vinaigrette, toss gently and let stand 10 minutes or more. Add remaining ingredients, toss gently and serve. Serves 4.

"The retreat was one hundred times more than I expected or imagined. First, it took place in an exquisite area of the Pacific Northwest, the Hood Canal on the Olympic Peninsula, in a town called Union. It was absolutely, breathtakingly beautiful. Second, the facilities could not have been more warm, welcome, conscious, and life-giving. Third, the food (yes, I am eating again!) was unbelievably delicious. Fourth, the program, the staff, and the overall commitment of Harmony Hill are nothing short of brilliant."

"'I came in despair and I left in hope."

"When I headed for home after the cancer retreat, I felt that I was going in the wrong direction. I've been back many times since then and the Harmony Hill programs always restore my positive outlook."

White Knight Salad

White foods such as cauliflower, celery, endive, garlic, leeks, mushrooms, and onions are anti-inflammatory and offer potent antioxidants that may help prevent cancers.

    1 cup white cabbage, cut into small florets
    2 stalks celery, chopped on diagonals
    1 head endive or Napa cabbage, shredded
    1 cup white mushroom caps, sliced
    Hot Onion Dressing (see below)

In a serving bowl, toss cabbage, celery, endive, and mushrooms, add dressing and serve. Serves 4–6.

Hot Onion Dressing

Also wonderful over baked potatoes, roasted vegetables, or grilled chicken.

    2 tablespoons virgin olive oil
    2 cloves garlic, chopped
    1 white or yellow onion, thinly sliced
    1/4 teaspoon salt
    1 tablespoon balsamic or cider vinegar
    1/4 teaspoon freshly ground black pepper

In a wide, shallow pan, heat oil and garlic over medium high heat until lightly golden (1–2 minutes). Add onion, sprinkle with salt, reduce heat to medium low and cook until soft and golden (8–10 minutes). Add balsamic vinegar and scrape bottom of pan gently to remove fond (the sticky bits). Sprinkle with pepper and serve hot. Makes about 1 cup (serves 4).

"I've never felt so safe and pampered. Our housemothers were supportive and staff so cheerful and an important asset to this experience. I am penniless and on welfare and this weekend was such a gift. I thank all who gave me this opportunity and feel so blessed and encouraged to finish my treatment."

3 Seasonal Soups

Almost every Harmony Hill menu includes soup. From winter's hearty potato or split pea soups to summer's spicy Italian tomato or sweet pepper bisque, there truly is a soup for every season. Ours often showcase homegrown ingredients such as runner beans and Gypsy peppers, rosemary and basil, edible nasturtiums and fragrant lavender.

Delicious, nutritious, and quick-cooking, soups make an easy, speedy main dish. Here's a simple soup "pattern" to spark your culinary creativity: Start with a little olive or canola oil and a member of the onion family (garlic, shallots, leeks, or red, white, green, or yellow onions). After a minute or two, add seeds (sesame, fennel, poppy, cumin), dried herbs, organic citrus zest, or fresh ginger.

Season to taste with fresh herbs, fresh citrus juices, salt, and pepper. Garnish soups with diced apples, shredded Savoy cabbage, sliced green onions, minced fennel, chopped almonds, or stemmed cilantro. To give soup body, add smoked paprika, vegetable broth powder, dry marsala, balsamic or rice vinegar, organic soy sauce (it has more depth), or anchovy paste (nobody ever guesses).

WINTER

Lentil and Split Pea Soup
Spicy Thai Fish Soup
Basque Black Bean Soup
Gardener's Chili

SPRING

Italian Leek and Lemon Soup
Fresh Pea Soup
French Sorrel Soup
Asparagus Soup

SUMMER

French Bean Soup with Orange
    and Lavender
Sweet Pepper Bisque
Roasted Tomato Soup
Gardener's Gazpacho

FALL

Sweet Potato Soup with
    Caramelized Pears
Chanterelle Soup
Spicy Gado-gado Soup
Corn Chowder
Potato Leek Soup

Tip To boost protein in soups, add thinly sliced chicken (simmer it for about 10 minutes), or shrimp, prawns, scallops, mussels, clams, or sliced fish, all of which cook in just 3–5 minutes. Vegetarians can add whisked eggs (2–3 per adult) that cook in 1–2 minutes, or tofu, which heats up just as fast.

Tip For a rich stock, use a cup or more of vegetables per person. Start with the most dense (such as carrots, potatoes, turnips), sauté for a minute or two, then add broth or water to cover. Cook the denser vegetables for 15–20 minutes, then add fresh peas, asparagus, leafy greens, green beans, zucchini, or tomatoes, which cook in 3–5 minutes.

Lentil and Split Pea Soup

During cooler months, this thick, hearty soup is one of our most-requested recipes. Vary the vegetables at your pleasure, and use a variety of fresh herbs for a change of pace.

> 1 teaspoon virgin olive oil
> 2 cloves garlic, chopped
> 1/2 teaspoon red pepper flakes
> 1 teaspoon cumin seed
> 1 onion, chopped
> 2 stalks celery, chopped
> 1 carrot, chopped
> 1 teaspoon ground cumin
> 1 teaspoon curry powder
> 1 cup split peas
> 1 cup green lentils
> 1 bay leaf (optional)
> 1/2 teaspoon salt
> 1/2 teaspoon smoked paprika or Tabasco® sauce

In a soup pot, heat oil, garlic, pepper flakes, and cumin seed over medium high heat and cook for 1–2 minutes. When fragrant, add onion, celery, carrot, ground cumin, and curry powder and cook for 2 minutes. Add 8 cups water, bring to a simmer, add split peas, lentils, and bay leaf (if using) and simmer until tender (20–30 minutes). Season with salt and smoked paprika and serve. Serves 8.

Spicy Thai Fish Soup

Outstanding on a chilly night! Harmony Hill uses fire-roasted tomatoes, sustainably harvested organic coconut milk, Mae Ploy Brand red curry paste, and Rufina fish sauce, but you can substitute freely.

30–35 ounces crushed tomatoes (fire-roasted preferred)
1/2 teaspoon red curry paste
2 tablespoons fish sauce
1 tablespoon lemon juice
8 ounces skinless white fish fillet, thinly sliced
1 can (about 1 1/2 cups) coconut milk
    (reduced fat works fine)
2 tablespoons cilantro, stemmed, or green onion, chopped

In a soup pot, bring tomatoes and 2 cups water to a simmer over medium high heat. Stir in red curry paste, fish sauce, and lemon juice, add fish and cook until opaque (3–5 minutes). Add coconut milk, reduce heat to low and simmer 5 minutes. Serve hot, garnished with cilantro or green onions. Serves 4.

Basque Black Bean Soup

Though extremely simple, Basque Black Bean Soup has a remarkably robust flavor. The quality of the beans makes all the difference, and locally grown beans taste best. If you can't find Basque Black beans, try Black Turtle or Black Coco beans.

2 cups raw Basque Black or any black beans
4 sweet carrots, chopped
1/2 teaspoon Italian seasoning herbs
    (rosemary, oregano, basil)
1/4 teaspoon Bragg Liquid Aminos or soy sauce
1/4 teaspoon freshly ground pepper
3 cloves garlic, chopped
1/4 cup Romano or Parmesan cheese, coarsely grated

Soak beans in 8 cups water overnight. Add water as needed to allow 1–2 inches above beans, add carrots, cover and cook until beans are tender (about an hour). Season to taste with Bragg or soy sauce and pepper. Puree half the soup with the garlic and return to pan. Heat through and serve, garnished with grated cheese. Serves 4–6.

Gardener's Chili

In the depths of winter, this rib-sticking vegetable chili has a vivid, citrusy flavor that reminds us of sunny days to come.

        1 teaspoon virgin olive oil
        4 cloves garlic, chopped
        3 organic oranges, juiced, rind grated
        1 red onion, chopped
        2 stalks celery, chopped
        1 turnip or parsnip, chopped
        2 cups Savoy or green cabbage, shredded
        4 cups Black Tuscan kale, shredded
        4 cups cooked or 2 cans (14–15-ounce) black beans
            (drained and rinsed if canned)
        1 can (28–32-ounces) crushed, fire-roasted
            tomatoes in sauce
        6-8 ounces salsa verde (green chile sauce)
        1 cup Napa cabbage, finely shredded
        2 satsumas, sectioned and chopped

Heat oil in a large sauce pan over medium high heat. Add garlic and orange rind and cook, stirring several times, until garlic is pale golden (3–4 minutes). Add onion, celery, and turnip and cook, stirring, until soft (4–5 minutes). Add cabbage and kale, cover pan and cook until barely wilted (2–3 minutes). Add beans and tomatoes and heat through (8–10 minutes). Stir in salsa verde, orange juice, and Napa cabbage, heat through (3–4 minutes) and serve, garnished with satsumas. Serves 6–8.

"On food: Terrific, packed full with love. All my dietary needs were more than met."

"Patients I send to Harmony Hill's Cancer Care Program come back transformed."

"This retreat was a life-saver for me. I was suffering from depression and anxiety. I feel 100% better after this weekend. Great support group."

Italian Leek and Lemon Soup

There are many versions of this healthful classic, but all are the Italian answer to spring colds or flu and delicious in their own right. For extra nutrition, add shreds of young kale and tender baby spinach greens.

2 teaspoons virgin olive oil
1 dried hot pepper (any kind)
6 cloves garlic, chopped
1 organic lemon, juiced, rind thinly sliced
    and finely chopped
1/2 teaspoon lemon thyme or any thyme, stemmed
4 leeks, thinly sliced (white and palest green parts only)
1/4 teaspoon kosher or sea salt
1/2 teaspoon freshly ground black pepper
6 cups vegetable or chicken broth
4 cups young kale, stemmed and shredded
4 cups young spinach, stemmed
2 tablespoons fresh garlic tips or chives, chopped
1/2 cup flat Italian parsley, stemmed

In a saucepan, heat oil over medium high heat. Add hot pepper, brown on all sides, then discard pepper. Add garlic, lemon rind, thyme, and leeks, sprinkle with 1/4 teaspoon each of salt and black pepper and cook, stirring often, until leeks are barely soft (6–8 minutes). Add broth, bring to a simmer. Add kale, spinach, and garlic tips or chives, cover pan and cook until lightly wilted (2–3 minutes). Add lemon juice to taste, starting with 2 teaspoons. Serve at once, garnished with parsley and remaining pepper. Serves 4.

"The opportunity to be at Harmony Hill made a huge difference in my life during this time of treatment."

Fresh Pea Soup

When the first baby peas arrive in garden or market, this delicate soup is a fitting celebration of spring. Silken tofu adds extra protein with very little fat.

   1 teaspoon unsalted butter
   1 teaspoon virgin olive oil
   4 green onions, thinly sliced
   1/4 teaspoon dried tarragon
   1/2 organic lemon, juiced, rind grated
   2 1/4 cups snow peas, ends trimmed, shredded
   2 cups fresh peas (shelled)
   1/4 teaspoon kosher or sea salt
   1/4 teaspoon smoked paprika
   1 quart chicken or vegetable broth
   12 ounces silken tofu (firm)
   1 tablespoon garlic greens or chives, chopped

In a soup pot, melt butter in oil over medium high heat. Add green onions, tarragon, and lemon rind and cook, stirring, for 2 minutes. Add 2 cups snow peas, reserving the rest for garnish. Cook, stirring, for 2 minutes. Add peas, sprinkle with salt and paprika, cover pan and cook until barely soft (2–3 minutes). Add 1 cup broth, tofu, and lemon juice and puree in batches in a food processor (15–20 seconds each). Return to pan with remaining broth, bring to a simmer (6–8 minutes) and serve, garnished with chives and chopped snow peas. Serves 4–6.

"A magnificent opportunity to be in 'a place apart' to both experience the community and to reflect on my own inner journey. The space is healing, the food is wholesome and delicious, the staff are welcoming, personal, and attentive, the facilitators are skillful, and the participants are gifts of love and spirit and steadfastness and humor and beauty and incalculable courage."

French Sorrel Soup

Tart and spunky as spring itself, this creamy green soup tastes especially good with hot, crusty garlic bread.

  1 teaspoon virgin olive oil
  2 shallots or 3 cloves garlic, chopped
  1 tablespoon mint, chopped
  2 cups French sorrel, shredded
  4 cups spinach, shredded
  1 quart chicken or vegetable broth
  1/4 teaspoon shoyu or soy sauce
  1/4 teaspoon Tabasco® sauce
  1 cup sour cream or quark (nonfat works fine)
  1/4 cup apple, finely chopped

In a soup pot, heat oil and shallots (or garlic) over medium high heat for 2 minutes. Add mint, sorrel, and spinach and cook, stirring, until lightly wilted (2–3 minutes). Add broth, bring to a simmer (5–6 minutes) and season with soy sauce and Tabasco®. Puree in batches in a food processor, return to pan, stir in sour cream. Heat through and serve, garnished with chopped apple. Serves 4–6.

"The tranquility and natural beauty of the surroundings helps peel off the layers of stress and enable immersion in the wonderful program. This weekend has rejuvenated my spirit. I feel stronger and more informed. I can go home and put some of this positive energy towards getting through my aggressive treatments and live a healthier life."

Asparagus Soup

The pure, sweet taste of early asparagus comes singing through this deceptively simple recipe. This is equally good with hop vine shoots or fiddleheads.

2 teaspoons butter
2 teaspoons fruity olive oil
2 tablespoons pine nuts or walnut pieces
3 cloves garlic, chopped
1 cup red onion, thinly sliced
1/4 teaspoon kosher or sea salt
6 cups asparagus, stem ends trimmed, chopped
1/4 teaspoon freshly ground black pepper

In a soup pot, melt butter in oil over medium high heat. Add nuts and 1 clove garlic and toast until crisp (1–2 minutes). Spoon nuts onto a plate, set aside. Add remaining garlic and onions, sprinkle with half the salt and cook, stirring, over medium heat for 15 minutes, set aside.

In the meantime, bring 6 cups water to a brisk boil with remaining salt, add asparagus and boil until barely tender (3–4 minutes). With a slotted spoon, remove asparagus to a food processor and blend with 2–3 cups cooking water to a smooth puree. Return puree to soup pot with onions and add additional cooking water to desired consistency. Serve hot, garnished with toasted nuts. Serves 4.

"Thank you for honoring my struggle by allowing me to be here, regardless of my ability to pay. It's very life-giving to take money out of the picture for all participants."

French Bean Soup
with Orange and Lavender

Fragrant lavender is Harmony Hill's signature flower. The blossoms may be used fresh or dried; for a similar impact, use about twice as much dried lavender as fresh.

> 1 teaspoon virgin olive oil
> 2 shallots, minced
> 1 organic orange, juiced, rind grated
> 2 teaspoons fresh, or 1 teaspoon dried, food-grade lavender
> 1 sweet orange or yellow pepper, chopped
> 1/2 cup grated carrot
> 1/4 teaspoon sea salt
> 2 skinless, boneless chicken breasts, in bite-sized pieces
> 1 quart chicken broth, hot
> 2 cups cooked white beans, rinsed and drained
>   (canned work fine)
> 3 cups spinach, finely shredded
> 1/2 teaspoon green peppercorns, drained
> 1/4 cup carrot curls (use a vegetable peeler)

In a pan, heat oil, shallots, orange rind, and lavender over medium high heat for 2 minutes. Add sweet pepper, carrot, and salt and cook for 2 minutes. Add chicken and cook, stirring, for 4 minutes. Add hot broth, cover pan and simmer over low heat until chicken is tender (15–20 minutes). Add beans and cook for 5 minutes. Add spinach, orange juice, and peppercorns, cover pan and cook until barely wilted (2–3 minutes). Serve hot, garnished with carrot curls. Serves 4.

Tip A rasp grater makes citrus rind easier to grate and use.

"Harmony Hill gave me my life back."

Sweet Pepper Bisque

Creamy and lush, this summer soup is surprisingly slim. Instead of adding cream, puree half of the soup, then combine the two halves and serve. (This works with any chunky soup.)

1 teaspoon virgin olive oil
2 cloves garlic, chopped
1/2 cup sweet onion, chopped
1/4 teaspoon kosher or sea salt
4 red or orange sweet peppers, seeded and chopped
1 quart chicken or vegetable broth, hot
1 teaspoon fresh tarragon or 1/4 cup fresh basil
1/4 teaspoon freshly ground black pepper
1/4 cup yogurt, sour cream, or quark (lowfat works fine)

In a soup pot, heat oil and garlic over medium heat and cook until soft (2–3 minutes). Add onion, salt, and peppers and cook, stirring, until slightly soft (3–5 minutes). Put in a food processor with 1 cup hot broth and puree until smooth. Stir into soup, add remaining broth, herbs, and pepper. Serve hot, garnished with yogurt or sour cream. Serves 4.

"This weekend was everything I hoped for and more. I came here hoping for clarity and peace; I'm leaving with a renewed sense of health and some really terrific new friends."

"One member of our group came with a wig on her head and left with the wig in her hands."

"I adore Harmony Hill—the people, the food, the labyrinths all create a healing retreat atmosphere of growth and love."

Roasted Tomato Soup

Slow-roasting improves even bland out-of-season tomatoes and brings out the fullest flavor in summer-ripe ones. At Harmony Hill, we use dense paste tomatoes such as Roma or Cascade, which don't dry out during cooking.

    1 quart (about 3 pounds) ripe tomatoes
    3 tablespoons fruity olive oil
    1/2 teaspoon kosher or sea salt
    1/2 teaspoon freshly ground black pepper
    2 teaspoons unsalted butter
    3 shallots or 6 cloves garlic, chopped
    2 large onions, chopped
    1 teaspoon lemon thyme (or any), minced
    1/4 teaspoon chipotle (or any) pepper flakes
    3 ripe tomatoes, chopped, or 3 cups canned diced
        tomatoes in juice
    1 quart chicken or vegetable broth, hot
    1 cup fresh basil, shredded

Preheat oven to 350 degrees F. Halve tomatoes lengthwise, rub with 2 tablespoons oil and arrange, cut side down, in a single layer on a rimmed baking sheet. Sprinkle with half the salt and pepper and bake at 350 until edges are lightly caramelized (40–45 minutes).

In a soup pot, melt butter in remaining oil over medium high heat. Add garlic, onions, thyme, and pepper flakes, sprinkle with remaining salt and cook, stirring often, until soft (5–6 minutes). Add fresh tomatoes, bring to a simmer, add broth and roasted tomatoes, including any pan juices. Puree in batches in a food processor (10–15 seconds each), return to pot, bring to a simmer and serve, garnished with fresh basil. Serves 6–8.

"The retreat weekend centered me and made it possible to bravely move on to the next step."

Gardener's Gazpacho

If you prefer this refreshing soup smooth, puree the whole thing in several batches before serving. Usually served chilled, it is most delicious at room temperature.

    2 cloves garlic, minced
    1/2 teaspoon salt
    4 cups ripe tomatoes, chopped (reserve juices)
    1 yellow bell pepper, seeded and chopped
    1 red bell pepper, seeded, diced
    2 stalks celery, chopped
    1 large cucumber, seeded and chopped
        (peel if thick-skinned)
    1 Walla Walla Sweet or Vidalia onion, chopped
    1/4 cup cider or balsamic vinegar
    1/2 teaspoon sugar
    1/2 teaspoon smoked paprika
    1 cup yellow cherry tomatoes, halved

In a food processor, combine the garlic and salt with half the tomatoes, peppers, celery, cucumber, and onion and puree for 1 minute. Combine puree in a serving bowl with remaining vegetables and season to taste with vinegar, sugar, and paprika. Serve at room temperature or chilled, garnished with cherry tomatoes. Serves 4–6.

"Wonderful! I felt so loved and 'at home.' I've cried, and I've relaxed. I've explored hidden emotions and I've learned meditative techniques I've so needed. I am so overwhelmed by the love and support! 'Thanks' is too small a word for this gift. When life as you know it has fallen apart, what a blessing to feel so loved and embraced—so nurtured. Because there is no charge, the gift is greater."

Sweet Potato Soup with Caramelized Pears

Lightly caramelized pears add a lingering, summery sweetness to this lush, sumptuous soup.

2 teaspoons virgin olive oil
2 teaspoons butter
3 shallots, chopped
1/2 teaspoon fennel or cumin seed
3 pears, peeled, cored, and chopped
1 large onion (2–3 cups), chopped
2 large sweet potatoes (4 cups), peeled and chopped
1/2 teaspoon kosher or sea salt
1/2 teaspoon sweet paprika
8 cups chicken or vegetable broth
1/4 cup sour cream (nonfat works fine)

Preheat oven to 400 degrees F. In a Dutch oven over medium high heat, combine oil and butter with shallots and fennel seed and cook until soft (4–5 minutes). Add pears, reduce heat to medium low and brown lightly on all sides. Add onions and sweet potatoes, sprinkle with 1/4 teaspoon each of salt and paprika, stir to coat and brown lightly (5–6 minutes). Cover pan and bake at 400 until potatoes are very soft (40–45 minutes). Puree in a food processor with 2–3 cups broth. Return to pan, add remaining broth, adjust seasoning and bring to a simmer over medium heat. Serve hot, garnished with sour cream. Serves 4–6.

"Harmony Hill has created a safe place to say the word 'cancer,' as well as a place to learn coping skills for this condition and for life."

Chanterelle Soup

In autumn, our woods are full of these golden, fluted, apricot-scented mushrooms. This simple soup brings out their delicate flavor perfectly.

　　2 tablespoons unsalted butter
　　2 cloves garlic, minced or pressed
　　1 large onion, chopped, or 2 leeks, finely sliced
　　2–3 cups chanterelles, finely sliced
　　1/4 teaspoon kosher or sea salt
　　1 quart chicken or vegetable broth
　　1 cup cooked brown or basmati rice

In a soup pot, melt butter over medium high heat, Add garlic and onions and cook until soft (3–5 minutes). Add mushrooms, sprinkle with salt, reduce heat to medium low, cover pan and cook until soft (6–8 minutes). Add broth and rice and simmer for 15–20 minutes. Serves 4–6.

"Thank you. Even people who have financial resources going into a cancer diagnosis can quickly find themselves paying incredible amounts for medicines and medical care, and find savings quickly depleted. Emotional and spiritual needs make way for life-saving medical needs—but they can make such a huge difference in the quality of life. Coming here has made me feel renewed—I go back with much more energy to face the continued battle. If we'd had to pay to attend, it would have been a hardship and we might have decided the money should be saved for the next prescription. Taking money out of the equation freed us to come without having to make that difficult choice."

Spicy Gado-gado Soup

When chilly breezes blow, we serve this Indonesian classic with its exotic combination of sweet potatoes, peanuts, and ginger. Real peanut butter (made only with peanuts and salt) delivers the best flavor.

> 2 teaspoons canola oil
> 2 cloves garlic, minced or pressed
> 1 1/2 inches ginger root, grated or minced
> 1/2 teaspoon smoked paprika or cayenne
> 1 large onion, chopped
> 1/8 teaspoon kosher or sea salt
> 1 pound sweet potatoes, peeled and chopped
> 1 quart chicken or vegetable broth
> 2 cups red cabbage, shredded
> 1/2 cup chunky real peanut butter
>   (just peanuts and salt)
> 2 ripe tomatoes, chopped, or 1 15-ounce can
>   diced tomatoes in juice
> 1 tablespoon mint, chopped
> 1 teaspoon shoyu or soy sauce
> 1/4 cup cilantro, stemmed
> 1/4 cup roasted peanuts, chopped

In a soup pot over medium high heat, cook oil, garlic, ginger, and smoked paprika for 2 minutes. Add onions, sprinkle with salt, and cook until soft (4–5 minutes). Add sweet potatoes, stir to coat and cook for 2 minutes. Add 3 cups broth, bring to a simmer, add cabbage, cover pan, reduce heat to low and simmer until tender (12–15 minutes). Thin peanut butter with remaining broth and stir slowly into hot soup. Add tomatoes and mint, season to taste with soy sauce. Heat through (3–5 minutes) and serve, garnished with cilantro and peanuts. Serves 4–6.

"The cancer programs gave me a new perspective and now I can deal with the effects of my cancer a lot better."

Corn Chowder

Serious Harmony Hill comfort food, this thick chowder is immediately satisfying, and leftovers taste even better when gently reheated.

2 teaspoons unsalted butter
2 teaspoons canola oil
4 cloves garlic, chopped
2 large onions, chopped
1/4 teaspoon salt
3 stalks celery, chopped
6 medium potatoes, diced (peeled unless organic)
1 quart milk (nonfat works fine)
1 tablespoon vegetable broth powder
1/4 cup whole wheat pastry flour (or any)
4 cups sweet corn, fresh, frozen, or canned (drained)
1/8 teaspoon freshly ground pepper
1 cup oyster crackers

In a soup pot, melt butter in oil over medium high heat. Add garlic, onions, and salt and cook for 3 minutes. Add celery and cook for 3 minutes. Add potatoes, milk, and vegetable broth powder, bring to a simmer, reduce heat to low, cover pan and simmer until tender (15–20 minutes). Blend flour with 1/3 cup cold water and stir slowly into hot soup. Simmer 3–5 minutes, add corn and pepper, heat through (3–4 minutes) and serve, garnished with crackers. Serves 4–6.

Tip To avoid lumps when thickening soups, stir the flour into cold water, then stir it slowly into the hot broth.

"Sometimes we feel so alone... The Harmony Hill retreat was a way to connect."

Potato Leek Soup

Nothing tastes better on a blustery winter night than the timeless combination of humble potatoes and autumn leeks. Picked after the first hard frost, leeks gain a subtle and pleasing sweetness.

2 teaspoons unsalted butter
2 teaspoons virgin olive oil
2 cloves garlic, finely chopped
1/2 teaspoon celery seed
1 large onion, chopped
1/4 teaspoon kosher or sea salt
2 cups leeks, thinly sliced (white and
    palest green parts only)
3 medium potatoes, peeled and diced
1 quart chicken or vegetable broth, hot
1/4 teaspoon freshly ground pepper
1/2 cup sour cream or yogurt (lowfat works fine)
2 tablespoons flat Italian parsley, stemmed,
    or chives, chopped

In a soup pot, melt butter in oil over medium high heat. Add garlic and celery seed and cook for 2 minutes. Add onion, sprinkle with salt and cook for 2 minutes. Add leeks and potatoes, stir to coat, cover pan and cook for 2 minutes. Add broth, bring to a simmer, reduce heat to low, cover pan and simmer until tender (15–20 minutes). Add pepper and serve, garnished with sour cream and parsley or chives. Serves 4–6.

"I needed this space—safe, warm, taken-care-of, to heal right now. I haven't had anyone lately in my life who could provide me with this. I am so deeply grateful for you all."

4 Seasonal Vegetarian Entrees

With encouragement from nutritionists and doctors, more of us are choosing to serve meatless meals more often. That's good for our health and good news for the planet, and it's also good news for food lovers. The Harmony Hill kitchen often opens people's eyes to the rich variety of plant-based foods; some guests can't believe our Tasty Taco Filling is meatless, while others on restricted diets are delighted to learn how delicious vegetarian meals can be.

Many cooks get flustered when new vegetarians enter the family picture. In large part, this is because vegetarian cooking is not as entrée-based as the average Western diet. Instead of serving a main dish and several sides, many traditional vegetarian cultures serve what seems like a series of sides. One way to ease into vegetarian cooking is to treat grains like pasta, serving them with sauces and zippy garnishes such as chopped cucumber, red onion, apple, or even melon, as well as fresh herbs or coarsely grated cheese. Casseroles, lasagna, and stuffed peppers or squash also make great transitional entrees.

Here are some introductory recipes to help you explore the possibilities. All look and taste great, promote health, reduce your carbon footprint, won't break your budget, and emphasize the freshest locally grown ingredients. Who could ask for more?

WINTER

Golden Lasagna
Spicy Polenta with Winter Greens
Peppery Winter Greens
Italian Spinach Pie
Stuffed Orange Peppers
Tasty Taco Filling
Taco Fixings

SPRING

Quinoa with Spring Greens
    and Dill Sauce
Dill Sauce
Red Risi Pisi
Primavera Slim
Spring Brunch Strata

SUMMER

Italian Fresh Tomato Pie
Sweet Corn and
    Cheddar Quesadillas
Hot Corn and Bean Salad
Hot Pasta Salad
Smoked Salmon Salad with
    Marionberry Dressing
Marionberry Dressing
Summer Salsa Soup

FALL

Chanterelle Omelet
Roasted Vegetable Pot Pie
    with Mushroom Gravy
Mushroom Gravy
No-Salt Herb Blend
Matsutake Mushrooms with
    Seasoned Rice
Sweet Dumpling Squash Cups

"There is no way we can possibly thank you for the opportunity to participate in the retreat last weekend. It was such a relief to simply get away from the whirlwind of doctor appointments, tests, and confounding news we have faced this last month. It seems strange to think that a weekend that has cancer as its focus could be called 'getting away' from cancer, but it really was. The genuine and deep caring that was expressed in every aspect of the gathering was beyond anything I could have imagined and I know I will be grateful for the experience through all that is to come. I know that I return with many new insights, a better grasp on myself and how I might look ahead to deal with the uncertainties awaiting me, and a sense of calm that is, at least in part, replacing the panic that was setting in before we came to Harmony Hill."

Golden Lasagna

One of Harmony Hill's most festive dishes, this fragrant, gorgeous neo-classic is always a huge hit with guests. To speed up the cooking, use frozen squash and no-boil lasagna noodles (just don't tell).

Filling
2 teaspoons unsalted butter
2 teaspoons virgin olive oil
1 large onion, chopped
4 cloves garlic, chopped
1/2 teaspoon kosher or sea salt
3 pounds acorn, winter, or butternut squash,
    peeled, seeded, and cut into 1" chunks,
    or 2 pounds frozen cubed winter squash
2 teaspoon fresh sage, finely chopped
2 teaspoons thyme, stemmed and chopped
1/4 teaspoon freshly ground black pepper
1 cup toasted hazelnuts or pecans, chopped

In a large shallow pan, melt butter in oil over medium high heat, add onion, garlic, and salt and cook until pale golden (8–10 minutes). Add squash and cook, stirring, until tender (12–15 minutes). Stir in sage, thyme, pepper, and nuts, set aside.

Cheese blend
2 cups fresh mozzarella, finely diced
3-4 ounces Romano, Asiago, or Parmesan cheese, grated

Toss gently, set aside.

"Harmony Hill has helped me to find a peaceful place in my heart and soul to prepare myself for surgery, radiation, and continuing the healing process in my life."

Sauce

1 tablespoon unsalted butter
2 tablespoons virgin olive oil
3 cloves garlic, minced or pressed
1/2 teaspoon kosher or sea salt
1/2 teaspoon hot pepper flakes
1/2 teaspoon nutmeg
1/4 teaspoon freshly ground black pepper
1/3 cup whole wheat pastry flour (or any)
4 cups milk (any) or 4 cups plain hazelnut or
    almond milk (sold in a box)
1 tablespoon anchovy paste (optional)

Melt butter in oil in a saucepan over medium high heat. Add
garlic, salt, pepper, and nutmeg and cook until fragrant (1–2
minutes). Stirring constantly with a fork or whisk, add flour
and cook for 2–3 minutes. Slowly whisk in milk, stirring
constantly until sauce thickens. Bring to a brisk simmer, add
anchovy paste (if using), reduce heat to low and simmer for
8–10 minutes. Remove from heat, set aside.

Noodles

1 box no-boil lasagna noodles
    or 12–14 lasagna noodles, cooked

Lightly oil a deep 3-quart baking pan or a 9- by 13-inch baking
pan and cover with noodles. Layer on 1/3 of the filling and 1/4
of the sauce and 1/4 of the cheese and repeat twice, ending with
noodles, sauce, and cheese. Cover pan with foil and bake at
400 degrees F until heated through (30–40 minutes). Remove
foil and bake until cheese is golden brown (10–15 minutes).
Remove from oven and let stand for 20–30 minutes before
serving. Serves 8–12.

---

*"Thank you for the nourishing wonderful food and the spirit
and goodwill surrounding it."*

Spicy Polenta
with Winter Greens

Creamy polenta is an Italian's idea of comfort food. It takes
a while to cook, so have something fun to read on hand while
stirring. Harmony Hill's spicy polenta can also be topped with
pasta sauce, cheese sauce, or Mushroom Gravy (see page 76)
for a satisfying meal.

> 1 tablespoon virgin olive oil
> 1 teaspoon hot pepper flakes (or less)
> 1 teaspoon fresh rosemary, chopped
> 1 teaspoon flat Italian parsley, chopped
> 3 cloves garlic, chopped
> 1 teaspoon salt
> 6 cups boiling water
> 2 cups coarse yellow cornmeal

In a saucepan, combine oil, pepper flakes, rosemary, parsley,
garlic, and salt over medium high heat and cook for 2 minutes.
Add boiling water and slowly stir in cornmeal. Reduce heat to
low, and cook, stirring frequently, until thick (25–30 minutes).
When polenta comes away from the side of the pan, pour into a
round, buttered bowl for 10 minutes, then unmold onto a plate
and serve, cut in wedges. Serves 6–8.

Peppery Winter Greens

Wonderful spooned over polenta, rice, or noodles.

> 1 tablespoon virgin olive oil
> 3 cloves garlic, minced
> 1/2 onion, chopped
> 1/4 teaspoon salt
> 3 cups Swiss chard or kale, chopped
> 3 cups mustard greens or collards, chopped
> 1 pound spinach, rinsed
> 1 can (4–6 ounces) green chiles, chopped
> 1/4 cup flat Italian parsley, stemmed
> 1/4 teaspoon freshly ground black pepper

In a wide, shallow pan, combine the oil, garlic, onions, and salt over medium high heat and cook for 3 minutes. Add the greens, cover pan and cook until wilted (5–7 minutes). Stir in the chiles and heat through (3–4 minutes). Serve hot over polenta, garnished with parsley and pepper. Serves 6–8.

Italian Spinach Pie

This traditional Torta Verde is simple to make and marvelously good for brunch, lunch, or dinner.

> 1 9-inch pie crust
> 10 ounces fresh spinach or 1 10-ounce box
>   frozen spinach, thawed and drained
> 1 pound ricotta (lowfat works fine)
> 1 large egg
> 1/2 teaspoon nutmeg (freshly grated is best)
> 1/2 teaspoon sea salt plus a pinch
> 1/4 teaspoon freshly ground black pepper
> 1/3 cup flour
> 2/3 cup Romano, Parmesan, or Asiago cheese, grated
> 2 teaspoons unsalted butter

Line a pie dish with crust and crimp edges, set aide. Drop spinach in boiling water and cook until wilted (2–3 minutes). Drain and press dry. (If frozen, drain and press dry only.) In a bowl, combine ricotta, spinach, egg, nutmeg, 1/2 teaspoon salt, and half the pepper and blend well. Stir in flour, then add 1/2 cup cheese. Spoon into pie shell, sprinkle with pinch of salt, remaining pepper, and remaining cheese, and dot with butter. Bake at 350 degrees F until puffed and nicely browned (40–45 minutes). Serve warm or at room temperature. Serves 6.

"If I had to pay for this, I would most likely not come. We have so many extra, new expenses while dealing with this diagnosis. Thank you dearly, this is a service like no other, a blessing, fodder for supporting my faith. I know this experience will benefit not only Ken and myself, but also our children, family, and community."

Stuffed Orange Peppers

Folks who don't get along with green peppers often find red, orange, or yellow ones more digestible. They're also sweeter and prettier than Plain Jane green ones, so experiment freely.

    4 orange sweet peppers, cored and seeded
    1 teaspoon virgin olive oil
    1 clove garlic, chopped
    1 organic orange, juiced, rind grated
    2 stalks celery, chopped
    2 cups baby spinach, stemmed
    4 cups fresh bread crumbs (any kind)
    6 green onions, thinly sliced
    1/2 cup wasabi-coated roasted almonds, chopped

Preheat oven to 350 degrees F. Drop peppers in a pot of boiling water and parboil for 3 minutes. Drain and set upright in a baking dish. In a wide, shallow pan over medium high heat, cook oil with garlic and orange rind until barely golden (2–3 minutes). Add celery and spinach and cook for 2 minutes. Add bread crumbs and green onions, cover pan and cook for 3 minutes. Add almonds and orange juice, stuff peppers with bread mixture and bake until hot through (about 30 minutes). Serve hot. Serves 4.

"We began as a group of strangers with one thing we knew we had in common: cancer. We ended our day as sisters. We shared our pain and lives and came away stronger. Our group will continue to stay in touch."

Tasty Taco Filling

Our guests never guess the secret ingredient and some will argue when you tell them this taco filling is meatless!

1 tablespoon virgin olive oil
1 cup onion, minced
1/2 cup celery, minced
2 cloves garlic, minced
1 cup red lentils (raw)
1 tablespoon medium chili powder
2 teaspoons ground cumin
1 teaspoon dried oregano, crumbled
2 cups vegetable broth
2 tablespoons raisins
1 cup medium (or any) salsa

In a wide, shallow pan, heat oil with onion, celery, and garlic over medium high heat for 5 minutes. Stir in lentils, chili powder, cumin, and oregano and cook for 1 minute. Add broth and raisins, cover pan, reduce heat to low and simmer until lentils are tender. Remove lid and cook, stirring, until mixture thickens. Stir in salsa and serve hot with taco fixings. Serves 8.

Taco Fixings

Set up as many of these as you have on hand—and whatever else tickles your fancy. Feeds 4 hearty or 8 light eaters.

8 corn tortillas (8–9-inch), warm
Tasty Taco Filling (see above)
2 cups lettuce, shredded
1 cup daikon radish sprouts, roots trimmed off
1/2 cup onion, chopped
1/2 cup radishes, sliced
1 cup cheddar cheese, grated
1 red or orange pepper, chopped
1 cup salsa
1/2 cup cilantro, stemmed
1/2 cup sour cream (nonfat works fine)
1 lime, cut in 8 wedges

Quinoa with Spring Greens and Dill Sauce

Fluffy, protein-rich quinoa is the perfect foil for the lively greens of spring. Rinse it well to remove bitter-tasting saponins, then shake dry before toasting with seeds.

> 1 teaspoon fennel seed
> 1 cup quinoa, well-rinsed
> 2 cups vegetable or chicken broth
> 1 teaspoon virgin olive oil
> 1/2 teaspoon dried hot pepper flakes
> 3 cloves garlic, chopped
> 1 leek, thinly sliced (about 1 cup)
> 1/4 teaspoon kosher or sea salt
> 10–12 ounces firm tofu, diced
> 2 cups mustard greens, finely shredded
> 2 cups red chard, finely shredded
> 2 cups Black Tuscan kale, finely shredded
> 1/4 cup grated Romano or Parmesan cheese
> Dill Sauce (see next page)
> 4 green onions, chopped

In a saucepan, dry toast fennel seed over medium high heat for 1 minute. Add quinoa and toast, stirring, for 2–3 minutes. Add broth, bring to a simmer, reduce heat to low and simmer over low heat until tender (15–20 minutes). Fluff with a fork, let stand 5 minutes. Meanwhile, in a wide, shallow pan, heat oil, pepper flakes, garlic, leeks, and salt over medium high heat and cook for 2 minutes. Add tofu and cook for 2 minutes. Add greens, cover pan and cook until wilted (3–5 minutes). Stir in cheese and heat through (1–2 minutes). Serve over hot quinoa with Dill Sauce, garnished with green onions. Serves 4.

Dill Sauce

This robust sauce complements grains or steamed vegetables.

1 tablespoon fresh dill, chopped
1 cup heavy cream or sour cream (nonfat works fine)
1/4 cup grated Romano or Parmesan cheese
1/4 teaspoon freshly ground pepper

Combine all ingredients and let stand for at least 15 minutes. Makes about 1 cup.

Tip If your garden lacks fresh herbs (or if you lack a garden), consider planting a pot of easy-going herbs to brighten up simple meals. A half-barrel can hold enough herbs to keep meals lively, as well as a Sungold cherry tomato plant or two. Flat Italian parsley, sage, rosemary, and lemon thyme can even be picked in winter, while basil and cilantro are warm-season annuals to replace every year.

"Thank you again for the fabulous week! I felt so nurtured and cared for during our stay. We've just returned home and unpacked, and I ran across all the wonderful gluten-free recipes you sent with us. Thank you for your generous spirit and kindness and for your sensitive attention to our needs. We were in heaven!

Your entire staff carries the spirit of cooperation and sincere caring and service, all the while moving seamlessly and effortlessly in carrying out the duties of the day. Having lived in community for ten years, I really sense the underlying commitment to service, love, and compassion that surrounds each person and the whole of Harmony Hill."

Red Risi Pisi

Italians love Risi Pisi, baby peas with rice in a lush cream sauce. Our version partners fast-cooking whole grain red rice with a melange of spring vegetables. If you don't have fresh pea vines, fennel greens make a fine substitute.

1 cup Bhutanese red rice or any rice
1/2 teaspoon kosher or sea salt
1/2 teaspoon freshly ground pepper
1 teaspoon butter
1 teaspoon virgin olive oil
2 shallots, finely chopped
1/4 teaspoon oregano
1 cup baby (2-inch) carrots, ends trimmed
1 cup Florence fennel, finely chopped
1/2 cup vegetable or chicken broth
1 cup fresh peas
1 tablespoon fresh chives, chopped
1/4 cup flat Italian parsley, stemmed
1/4 cup fresh fennel foliage, stemmed
1/2 cup heavy cream or plain yogurt (nonfat works fine)
1/4 cup fresh pea tendrils or fennel greens

Cook rice according to package directions, adding half the salt and pepper. Meanwhile, in a wide, shallow pan, heat butter in oil over medium high heat. Add shallots, remaining salt and pepper, and oregano and cook, stirring, until soft (2–3 minutes). Add carrots, fennel, and broth, bring to a simmer, cover pan and cook until tender (4–6 minutes). Add peas and simmer, uncovered, until barely tender (1–2 minutes). Add fresh herbs, cook 1 minute, stir in cream and serve over hot rice, garnished with pea tendrils. Serves 4.

"I am so grateful to be here this weekend, my spirit is lifted. I feel my heart has been so happy, my body is weak and hurting but I feel joy."

Cooking at Harmony Hill

Primavera Slim

Serve this slimmed-down primavera sauce over whole grain pasta, quinoa, or wild rice to boost flavor, protein, and fiber. Thick, tangy quark (similar to sour cream) thickens the sauce, and the garnish of Parmesan curls melts delectably in the mouth. Delicioso!

10–12 ounces whole grain pasta (fettuccine or any)
1 teaspoon virgin olive oil
3 cloves garlic, chopped
1 white or yellow onion, chopped
10 ounces brown mushrooms, thinly sliced
1/4 teaspoon kosher or sea salt
1/4 teaspoon freshly ground black pepper
1 cup dry white wine or broth
1 cup fresh peas
1 cup asparagus, stems snapped, cut in 1-inch pieces
1 teaspoon fresh oregano, stemmed
1 teaspoon fresh thyme, stemmed
2 teaspoons capers, drained
1 cup quark or sour cream (nonfat works fine)
1–2 ounces Parmesan curls (use a vegetable peeler)

Start water for pasta and cook according to package directions. In a wide, shallow pan, heat oil and garlic over medium high heat for 2 minutes. Add onion and cook, stirring, until pale golden (3–4 minutes). Add mushrooms, sprinkle with salt and pepper, cover pan and sweat until juices run (2–3 minutes). Add wine, bring to a simmer, reduce heat to low and simmer until liquid is reduced by half (6–8 minutes). Add peas, asparagus, herbs, and capers, cover pan and cook until tender (2–3 minutes). Stir in quark and serve over hot, drained pasta, garnished with cheese curls. Serves 4.

"I can come here and say the 'C' word without worrying about others' reactions. I can face it instead of ignoring it."

Spring Brunch Strata

Next time you have extra rice or quinoa on hand, make Spring Brunch Strata, an easier version of the classic rice frittata that offers plenty of protein and tastes great warm or cold.

    2 cups cooked wild, black, or brown rice or cooked quinoa
    4 cups milk
    6 eggs, beaten
    1/2 teaspoon kosher or sea salt
    1/4 teaspoon freshly ground black pepper
    1 teaspoon virgin olive oil
    2 cloves garlic, chopped
    1 bulb fennel with greens, chopped
    4 heads baby bok choy with leaves, chopped
    12 spears asparagus, ends snapped, cut in 1-inch pieces
    20 sugar snap pea pods, cut in 1-inch pieces
    4 cups spinach, stemmed
    1 teaspoon oregano, stemmed
    1 cup feta cheese, crumbled (or any)

Pat rice evenly in a deep 9- by 13-inch baking dish. Whisk milk and eggs together with half the salt and pepper, set aside. In a wide, shallow pan, heat oil over medium high heat with garlic and fennel and cook, stirring, for 2 minutes. Add bok choy and asparagus and cook, stirring, until barely tender (2–3 minutes). Add pea pods and spinach, sprinkle with oregano and remaining salt and pepper, cover pan and cook until spinach is barely wilted (1–2 minutes). Layer cooked vegetables over rice, sprinkle with cheese, pour egg mixture over the top and refrigerate overnight or all day. Bake at 350 degrees F until set, puffed, and golden (35–45 minutes). Serves 8–10.

"I believe this retreat is a turning point in my journey and a powerful new light that carries within an abundance of hope."

Italian Fresh Tomato Pie

Redolent with tomatoes and fresh basil, this classic Torta di Pomidori is one of summer's most delicious dishes.

1 9-inch pie crust
4 cups sliced ripe tomatoes
1/2 cup fresh basil, stemmed and shredded
1/4 teaspoon kosher or sea salt
2 teaspoons capers, drained
1/4 cup fresh bread crumbs (1 slice, grated
     in food processor)
1 tablespoon fresh flat Italian parsley, chopped
1/2 teaspoon fresh oregano, stemmed and chopped
1/4 teaspoon freshly ground black pepper
1 red onion, cut in half and thinly sliced
4-6 ounces goat cheese, crumbled

Line a 9-inch pie dish with crust, crimp edges, set aside. Gently toss tomatoes with basil, 1/8 teaspoon salt, and capers and set aside. Blend bread crumbs with parsley, oregano, remaining salt, and pepper, set aside. Layer tomato mixture and red onion into pie shell, alternating with (and ending with) bread crumb mixture. Top with crumbled goat cheese and bake at 400 degrees F until hot through (20–25 minutes). Serve warm or at room temperature. Serves 4–6.

"The one thing I was so looking forward to was meeting other folks with cancer diagnoses. As it turned out, our group included those who were recently diagnosed, others who had just completed their treatments, others who were cured, and others who were diagnosed as terminal. To be amongst this group, share our thoughts and experiences with one another, laugh and cry, and generally explore what is next together was an incredibly valuable experience that just continues to resonate with me. Bottom line: the Harmony Hill Retreat Center and its cancer programs are one of the biggest gifts I have ever received in my life. THANK YOU, HARMONY HILL!"

Sweet Corn
and Cheddar Quesadillas

Pan-toasted or baked, these quesadillas cook fast, keeping the summer kitchen cool. You can also wrap them in foil and grill for 2–3 minutes per side. For a change of pace, try Pepper Jack, smoked mozzarella, or fresh goat cheese.

8 corn tortillas (8–9-inch)
4-6 ounces extra sharp cheddar (or any), coarsely grated
1/4 cup Walla Walla Sweet onions, chopped
1 ear sweet corn, kernels trimmed
1/4 cup cilantro, stemmed

To bake, place 4 tortillas on a baking sheet, top with half the cheese and all the onions, corn, and cilantro, top with remaining cheese and tortillas and bake at 350 degrees F until hot (5–6 minutes). Flip and bake for 3 minutes, then serve.

To pan-fry, heat an iron skillet (dry, no oil) over medium high heat. Add a corn tortilla, top evenly with 2 tablespoons cheese and cook for 30 seconds. Add onions and cilantro, sprinkle with 1 tablespoon cheese, top with another tortilla and flip. Cook for 30 seconds or until cheese melts. Remove to plate in warm oven and repeat process three more times. Makes 4.

"Just being reminded that I'm not alone or the only one [with cancer] is more valuable than words can say. My needs were met, my soul rejuvenated, and I was thankfully introduced to non-pretzel yoga! Thank you, thank you, thank you! This weekend, while short, is not only life-saving but life-enriching. Cancer can be a very isolating disease, and being able to share time with those who share some small part of your experience is so powerful and healing that words can't do it justice. I have healed in ways I didn't think would ever be possible. The staff is phenomenal and the experience was just amazing."

Hot Corn and Bean Salad

For fullest flavor, use roasted red or yellow peppers, white or bicolor sweet corn, fresh oregano and basil, and juicy heirloom tomatoes. Leftovers make a fabulous omelet stuffing.

> 1 red or yellow sweet pepper, seeded and sliced
> 1 teaspoon cumin seed
> 1/4 teaspoon kosher or sea salt
> 1 teaspoon virgin olive oil
> 1 clove garlic, chopped
> 1/2 cup Walla Walla Sweet onion, chopped
> 2 ears sweet corn, kernels cut
> 1 cup string beans, tipped and chopped
> 2 cups cooked pinto beans or 1 15-ounce can
>   pinto beans, rinsed and drained
> 2 cups Mortgage Raiser or any heirloom tomato,
>   diced (with juice)
> 1 teaspoon fresh oregano, stemmed
> 1 tablespoon cider vinegar
> 1/4 cup basil, shredded

In a heavy iron skillet, roast peppers, cumin seed, and salt over medium high heat until slightly singed (4–5 minutes). Add oil and garlic and cook for 2 minutes. Add onion, corn, and string beans and cook until corn starts to darken (3–4 minutes). Add pinto beans, tomatoes, and oregano, reduce heat to low and cook until warmed through (3–4 minutes). Add vinegar, heat for 1 minute and serve, garnished with basil. Serves 4.

"I am still on cloud nine from my weekend here. I am so rejuvenated, rested, and content. Thanks so much to you and all the staff for your nurturing. Harmony Hill will be a memory I will never forget."

Hot Pasta Salad

Use any favorite fresh tomato, and add fresh chives if you like.

12–16 ounces whole grain pasta
2 cups Sungold grape tomatoes, halved
2 cups Black Prince grape tomatoes, halved
1/2 cup fresh basil, shredded
1/4 teaspoon kosher or sea salt
1/4 teaspoon freshly ground black pepper
1/2 cup Kalamata or Niçoise olives, stoned and chopped
2 tablespoons pine nuts or chopped almonds
4–6 ounces fresh goat cheese or feta, crumbled
2 green onions, finely chopped

Cook pasta according to package directions, reserving about 1/2 cup cooking water. Do not halt cooking with cold water when done. While pasta cooks, combine tomatoes, basil, salt, pepper, and olives. In a serving bowl, gently toss drained, hot pasta with goat cheese and pine nuts, adding cooking water by the tablespoon to make a creamy sauce. Add tomato mixture, toss gently and serve, garnished with green onions. Serves 4.

"I live in a rural area with few resources for follow-up after initial treatments. Therefore, help on the journey after cancer and even survival is facilitated by Harmony Hill. Thank you!"

"Thank you for making this possible. We would love to come back again, we gained a sense of peace within ourselves. As a couple, we understand each other's feelings and emotions better and we closer to one another."

"It nourishes my mind and soul so there is strength in my healing journey."

Smoked Salmon Salad
with Marionberry Dressing

Feel free to substitute tempeh (smoked tofu) for the salmon, or add one sliced, hard-boiled egg for each serving.

    2 cups young local greens
    1 cup fresh spinach, stemmed and shredded
    1 cup green cabbage, finely shredded
    1 cup arugula or mustard greens, shredded
    8–12 ounces soft smoked salmon, skinned, or 8-12
        ounces tempeh, sliced, or 4 hard-boiled eggs, sliced
    1/2 Walla Walla Sweet onion, diced
    1 cup fresh tomatoes, diced
    1 peach or nectarine, diced
    2 stalks celery, finely sliced
    1/4 cup cilantro, stemmed
    1/4 cup smoked almonds, chopped

Divide ingredients among four dinner plates and serve at room temperature, garnished with smoked almonds and accompanied by Marionberry Dressing (see below). Serves 4.

Marionberry Dressing

Try this sweet-tart dressing over greens, steamed vegetables, or grilled fish.

    1 cup fresh Marionberries, mashed
    1 teaspoon sugar or honey
    1 shallot, minced or pressed
    1/2 teaspoon lemon thyme or any thyme,
        stemmed and chopped
    1/8 teaspoon salt
    1/8 teaspoon freshly ground black or white pepper
    1/4 cup virgin olive oil
    2–3 tablespoons balsamic vinegar

Combine all ingredients in a food processor and puree for 10–15 seconds. Makes about 1 cup. Refrigerate for up to 5 days.

Summer Salsa Soup

Like gazpacho, this chunky garden soup celebrates summer garden bounty (puree the whole thing if you prefer a smoother soup). Use any assortment of vegetables you like, combining sweet and hot peppers to suit your taste.

1 organic lime, juiced
1 clove garlic, minced or pressed
1/4 cup cilantro, stemmed
1 tablespoon mint, stemmed and chopped
1 tablespoon Italian parsley, stemmed and chopped
1/8 teaspoon salt
2 cups ripe red tomatoes, diced
1 Jalapeno or Ancho chile pepper, seeded and chopped
    (use gloves!)
4 cups vegetarian broth or V-8® juice
4 cups Sungold or any yellow cherry tomatoes, cut in half
2 red bell peppers, seeded and chopped
1/2 Walla Walla Sweet onion, chopped
1 cup tomatillos, husked and cut in half
1 ripe avocado, diced

In a food processor, combine lime juice, garlic, herbs, salt, diced tomatoes, and chile pepper and puree to a coarse slurry. Add 1 cup broth and half the tomatoes, red peppers, onion, and tomatillos and puree for 30 seconds. In a serving bowl, combine with remaining ingredients, stir gently and serve at room temperature, garnished with avocado. Serves 4.

"This was a valuable experience and essential tool to add to my toolbox. There were no worries of how to afford it, so all focus could be given to the healing. I came feeling empty and leave here feeling full, with a whole new group of friends. My garden is in full bloom!"

Cooking at Harmony Hill

Chanterelle Omelet

The woods near Harmony Hill hold a treasure-trove of seasonal treats, including delicious chanterelles. This puffy, ricotta-enhanced omelet is also delightful with Crimini, shaggy mane, or morel mushrooms.

   3 eggs, lightly beaten
   1/4 cup ricotta (lowfat works fine)
   1 teaspoon virgin olive oil
   2–3 (about 1 cup) white or golden chanterelles,
      thinly sliced
   1/2 green bell pepper, thinly sliced
   2 green onions, chopped
   1/8 teaspoon kosher or sea salt
   1 teaspoon butter
   2 tablespoons fresh goat cheese, crumbled

In a bowl, combine eggs with ricotta, blend well with a fork, set aside. In a shallow, wide omelet or frying pan over medium high heat, combine oil, mushrooms, green pepper, and onions. Sprinkle with salt and cook until tender (3–5 minutes). Remove to a plate. Add butter to pan, heat until foamy, then pour in egg mixture and swirl to coat pan. Shake pan lightly, then gently pull back cooked eggs with a spatula to allow runny, uncooked portion to run underneath the cooked part. When center of omelet is lightly set (about 1 minute), cover half the eggs with mushroom mixture and top with goat cheese. Gently fold omelet in half, slide onto a plate, and serve hot. Serves 2.

"Harmony Hill is a safe and nourishing place where everyone is welcomed and loved. It's like a really awesome 'day care' for the cancer survivor's soul."

Roasted Vegetable Pot Pie with Mushroom Gravy

Our kitchen staff creates dried herb blends of many kinds. For roasted autumn vegetables, we like the salt-free one on the facing page, but feel free to use your own favorite combination.

  2 tablespoons virgin olive oil
  6 cloves garlic, chopped
  2 tablespoons No-Salt Herb Blend (see next page)
  3 large parsnips, peeled and chopped
  3 small turnips, peeled and chopped
  4 large carrots, peeled and chopped
  1 rutabaga, peeled and chopped
  1 sweet potato, peeled and chopped
  3 potatoes, peeled and chopped
  1 batch Mushroom Gravy (see below)
  1 9-inch pie crust

Preheat oven to 425 degrees F. Combine oil, garlic, and No-Salt Herb Blend in a large roasting pan, toss vegetables to coat evenly and roast until tender (40–50 minutes). Place vegetables in a deep pie dish or round casserole, cover with mushroom gravy and top with crust, crimping edges. Lower oven to 400 degrees F and bake until crust is golden (30–35 minutes). Serve with a big spoon rather than in slices. Serves 6–8.

Mushroom Gravy

Try this over boiled noodles, or spoon it over grilled Portobello mushrooms on toast and serve as a hot sandwich.

  1/4 cup unsalted butter
  2 Portobello mushrooms, finely diced
  1 cup dry red wine
  2 cups vegetable broth
  1/4 cup flour

In a wide, shallow pan, melt butter over medium high heat, add mushrooms and cook until barely tender (6–8 minutes).

Add wine and simmer to reduce (8–10 minutes). Blend broth and flour until smooth, then whisk flour mixture into hot wine, stirring constantly until thick. Thin as desired with water or broth. Makes about 3 cups.

No-Salt Herb Blend

Terrific in soups and on leafy salads, this enlivening seasoning mixture is also excellent on steamed or roasted vegetables, savory fruit salads, and omelets.

3 organic oranges, rind grated
3 organic lemons, rind grated
10 large cloves garlic, thinly sliced
1/4 cup dried lemon thyme or any thyme
2 tablespoons dried rosemary
2 tablespoons dried marjoram
1 tablespoon dried sage
1 tablespoon dried oregano
1 tablespoon (or less) dried hot pepper flakes
1/4 cup ground black pepper (or less)
1 teaspoon sweet paprika

Mix all ingredients and store in a sealed glass jar. When dry, mixture may be ground finer in a blender if desired. Makes about 1 cup.

"A cancer diagnosis is a traumatic experience for a family. Coming to a program that works to heal the mind is a very necessary step in the recovery process. This weekend has given me mental tools to face whatever comes in the future."

Matsutake Mushrooms with Seasoned Rice

Distinctively spicy and fragrant, our native Northwestern matsutake or pine mushrooms have a unique flavor that some liken to cinnamon. To let that remarkable flavor shine through, our simple version of the Japanese classic recipe uses ponzu (a Japanese dipping sauce with several forms) and plain tofu instead of soy sauce, sake, and fried tofu.

    1 cup Japanese rice
    1–2 (about 2 cups) matsutake mushrooms
    1 cup firm tofu, thinly sliced
    1 tablespoon ponzu vinegar or plain rice vinegar
    1 teaspoon ponzu soy sauce or any soy sauce

Rinse rice until water runs clear, drain. Combine rice with 1 cup water in a rice cooker or saucepan and let stand for 30 minutes. Brush mushrooms clean, peel the stems, and slice thinly lengthwise. Add mushrooms, tofu, and ponzu to the rice, cover lid and start rice cooker. (If using saucepan, bring to a boil over high heat, reduce heat to low, cover pan and cook until tender, about 20 minutes.) Serves 4.

"This has been an incredible experience! I have totally kept all these feelings in, bottled up for 13 years and 2 diagnoses of breast cancer. I feel relieved. Lifted. At ease with myself for the first time in years. For 13 years, I have been an exclusive member of the 'cancer club' and am finally and just now able to meet tons of the other members. How cool is that! Thank you so much for this opportunity!"

Sweet Dumpling Squash Cups

When autumn's bounty fills the kitchen, we love to serve these beautiful golden cups, loaded with apples, nuts, and cheese.

    2 Sweet Dumpling or Acorn squash, cut in half and seeded
    1 cup cooked white navy beans or 1 15-ounce can white
        navy beans, rinsed and drained
    1 cup tempeh or firm tofu, diced
    1 McIntosh or Macoun apple, cored and diced
    1 organic orange, juiced, rind grated
    1/4 teaspoon kosher or sea salt
    2 teaspoons capers, drained (optional)
    1/4 cup cilantro, stemmed (optional)
    1 teaspoon green peppercorns, drained (optional)
    1/4 cup roasted hazelnuts or cashews, chopped
    1 cup Jack or fresh mozzarella cheese, grated

Preheat oven to 350 degrees F. Place squash, cut side down, in a baking dish with 1 inch of water. Bake at 350 until soft (30–45 minutes). In a bowl, combine beans and tofu with apples, orange juice and rind, salt, capers, cilantro, and green peppercorns. When squash is tender, turn cups over and fill with bean and tofu mixture, topping each with hazelnuts and grated cheese. Return to oven and bake until warmed through (15–20 minutes). Serve hot. Serves 4.

"I am extremely grateful for this nourishing, relaxing, heart-felt experience that was offered to us with 'no strings attached.' It truly felt like a gift. It was easier to be open and accepting without the baggage of paying for it or feeling the need to be 'getting your money's worth.' The gift came from the heart and really felt like that."

5 Seasonal Seafood Entrees

Located on the bountiful Hood Canal, Harmony Hill's kitchen is full of fresh seafood, from the famous Dungeness crab to scallops, shrimp, clams, and more. Our Northwestern salmon is justly famed as a delicious and generous source of beneficial omega-3 oils, while the tender little Olympia oysters are world-famous.

Many guests say they enjoy seafood but don't know how to cook it. To get comfortable with fish and seafood, start with simple recipes that feature just a few fresh ingredients. Fast cooking times make fish a fabulous choice when time is tight. If you aren't sure whether fish is done, poke it gently—cooked fish flakes easily and is barely opaque all the way through.

The American Cancer Society recommends eating a variety of fish and other seafood on a regular basis. If your family considers seafood to be bland and tasteless, recipes like Peachy Chipotle Prawns and Lemon Zinger Sole will help change their minds.

These recipes can be altered freely by switching herbs and spices and changing fish and vegetables seasonally. Those with shellfish allergies may always substitute another kind of fish or even use lean poultry or tofu instead of a troublesome ingredient.

WINTER

Cranberry Salmon with Ginger
 Mango Chutney
Prawns and Scallops with
 Parsnips and Leeks
Pepper Lime Halibut
Sesame Shrimp Saute
Poached Salmon with Greens
 and Oranges

SPRING

Lemon Zinger Sole
Penne with Tuna, Asparagus,
 and Mushrooms
Springtime Salmon Salad
Springtime Ginger Dressing

SUMMER

Grilled Salmon with Lavender
 and Basil
Garlic Shrimp
Hot Tuna Salad
Peachy Chipotle Prawns
Pasta with Summery Clam Sauce

FALL

Scallops with Matsutake
 Mushrooms
Grilled Arctic Char with Apple
 Lime Salsa
Apple Lime Salsa
Marinated Tilapia with Smoked
 Tomato Dressing
Smoked Tomato Dressing
Salmon with Black Bean Sauce
 and Cilantro
Baked Mackerel
Trout with Red Grapes and Ginger

Tip Cooking fish in covered pans, over relatively low heat, releases moisture. Indeed, most fish contains so much moisture that a small amount of butter and citrus juice, combined with the fish's own "juice," makes plenty of poaching liquid. Adding vegetables and letting them braise in their own juice is another way to intensify the flavors of mild fish, as you'll see in this chapter.

Tip An instant-read thermometer makes cooking seafood a breeze. When fish, scallops, shrimp, or clams reach 136 degrees F, they are safely cooked. Let them stand (tented with foil or an inverted plate) for an additional 5–10 minutes before serving.

Cranberry Salmon
with Ginger Mango Chutney

We love recipes that cook quickly yet taste extraordinary. This one also works fine with rainbow trout or snapper.

> 1 1/2 pounds salmon fillet, cut in six pieces
> 1/4 cup fresh ginger, coarsely grated
> 2 organic oranges, juiced, rind grated
> 1/4 teaspoon kosher or sea salt
> 2 cups cranberries
> 1 red or sweet onion, chopped
> 2 ripe mangoes, peeled, pitted, and sliced
> 2–3 tablespoons Grade B maple syrup

Place salmon in a wide, shallow pan and sprinkle with 1 tablespoon ginger, 1 teaspoon orange rind, and 1/8 teaspoon salt. Add 1/3 cup orange juice and 1 cup cranberries, cover pan, bring to a simmer over medium high heat, reduce heat to low and cook until fish is opaque (136 degrees F) and cranberries have popped. Remove fish to a serving platter and tent with foil. Add to the pan the onions, three-fourths of the mango, 2 tablespoons maple syrup, the remaining cranberries, ginger, and orange juice and rind and cook until soft (5–6 minutes). Season to taste with maple syrup and salt and serve with fish, garnished with remaining mango. Serves 4–6.

"Thanks so much. Being able to learn coping skills and sharing experiences with others in a similar situation was valuable to my own journey with cancer."

Prawns and Scallops
with Parsnips and Leeks

Also excellent with small Japanese white turnips or with golden beets. Organic root vegetables always offer the fullest flavor and most antioxidants.

    1 teaspoon virgin olive oil
    2 cloves garlic, chopped
    1 organic orange, rind grated, juiced
    1 parsnip, peeled and chopped (2–3 cups)
    1 large leek, finely sliced (2–3 cups)
    1/4 teaspoon kosher or sea salt
    8–12 ounces peeled, deveined prawns
    8–12 ounces bay scallops
    2–3 tablespoons chili ponzu or salsa

In a heavy frying pan, combine oil, garlic, orange rind, and parsnips over medium high heat. Cook, stirring occasionally, until lightly seared (3–4 minutes). Add leeks, sprinkle with salt, stir to coat, cover pan and cook until vegetables weep juices (5–6 minutes). Add orange juice, reduce heat to medium low and cook, covered, until tender (10–15 minutes). Stir in prawns and scallops, cover pan and cook for 2 minutes. Stir, turning all prawns and scallops, and cook until opaque (2–3 minutes). Season to taste with chili ponzu, let stand off heat for 5 minutes, and serve over rice. Serves 4–6.

"Harmony Hill food is tremendously creative."

"Food: absolutely amazing. Healthy comfort food."

"I would compare your preparations and quality of food to a five-star restaurant."

Pepper Lime Halibut

Unlike its East Coast cousin, Pacific halibut is sustainably caught and can be enjoyed frequently. This recipe also works well with trout, salmon, or snapper, and you can scale the recipe up or down with ease.

1 1/2 pounds Pacific halibut fillet, cut in six pieces
1 organic lime, juiced, rind grated
1/8 teaspoon kosher or sea salt
1/4 teaspoon freshly ground black pepper
1/4 teaspoon coriander, cinnamon, or cumin
1 lime, cut in wedges

Place fish, skin side down, in a wide, shallow pan and sprinkle with lime rind, salt, and pepper. Spritz with lime juice (use it all), sprinkle with cinnamon, cover pan and bring to a simmer over medium high heat. Reduce heat to low and cook until fish is opaque (136 degrees F, about 8–9 minutes). Remove fish to a serving platter, leaving skin behind, and tent with foil for 5 minutes. Serve with a lime wedge. Serves 6.

Sesame Shrimp Saute

One of the oldest seasonings in the history of the kitchen, sesame seeds are recognized today as a good source of minerals as well as of cholesterol-lowering lignins. Here, they give sizzling, gingery shrimp a toasty twist.

2 teaspoons vegetable oil
4 cloves garlic, chopped
1 inch ginger, finely chopped
2 tablespoons sesame seeds
1 onion, thinly sliced
2 stalks celery, thinly sliced on the diagonal
1 red or yellow bell pepper, thinly sliced
1 pound peeled, deveined shrimp
1/4 teaspoon shoyu or soy sauce

In a wide, shallow pan, cook oil, garlic, ginger, and sesame seeds over medium high heat for 2 minutes. Add onion, celery, and pepper and cook, stirring, for 3 minutes. Cover pan and cook until tender (2–3 minutes). Add shrimp and cook for 2 minutes, flip and cook until opaque (2–3 minutes). Sprinkle with soy sauce and serve hot. Serves 4.

Poached Salmon
with Greens and Oranges

Ready in minutes, this beautiful dish showcases salmon's buttery, velvety texture and tastes both fresh and subtle.

  1 pound skinless salmon fillet, cut in four pieces
  2 organic oranges, rind grated
  1/4 teaspoon sea salt
  1/4 teaspoon freshly ground black pepper
  2 cups Black Tuscan kale or collards, shredded
  4 cups spinach, rinsed
  4 green onions, thinly sliced

Arrange salmon in a wide, shallow pan and sprinkle with half the orange zest, salt, and pepper. Juice one orange and add juice to pan. Cut peel from remaining orange, section and chop, set aside. Bring to a boil over medium high heat. Reduce heat to low, cover pan and simmer until fish is opaque (136 degrees F, about 8 minutes). Remove fish to serving plates and tent lightly with foil. Add kale to pan, cover and cook until barely tender (3–5 minutes). Add spinach, oranges, and remaining zest, salt and pepper, cover pan and cook until barely tender (2–3 minutes). Spoon over fish and serve, garnished with green onions. Serves 4.

"A wonderful, serene setting. Warm atmosphere. Excellent food. It was prepared with much thoughtfulness and love."

Lemon Zinger Sole

Stacking skinny fillets gives these fragile fish better integrity in the pan; they hold their shape nicely and the vivid, lemon-pepper pan sauce makes them pleasantly memorable.

 1 1/4 pounds sole fillets, cut in 3-inch pieces
 1/4 teaspoon kosher or sea salt
 1/4 teaspoon freshly ground black pepper
 2 teaspoons unsalted butter
 1 clove garlic, chopped
 1 tablespoon lemon juice

In a small shallow pan, stack fish in four equal piles, sprinkling with salt and pepper. Dot pan with butter and garlic, spritz fish with lemon juice (use it all), cover pan and bring to a simmer over medium high heat. Reduce heat to low and simmer until fish is opaque (internal temperature of 136 degrees F, about 7–8 minutes). Remove from heat and let stand for 5 minutes. Serve hot, with pan sauce spooned over each stack. Serves 4.

"I don't know the words that could really say it, I am so grateful. I live on less than $600 a month. If you hadn't provided financial support for this retreat so I could go... It is healing for body, mind, and soul—the place and the people and the program."

Penne with Tuna, Asparagus, and Mushrooms

For a vegan version, replace the tuna with smoked tempeh, cut in thin strips. At Harmony Hill, we might use morels picked under our towering fir trees in spring or woodland chanterelles or matsutake mushrooms in fall.

  8–10 ounces penne noodles
  1 tablespoon pine nuts
  1 tablespoon virgin olive oil
  3 cloves garlic, chopped
  1 teaspoon rosemary, stemmed and chopped
  4 large Crimini mushrooms, caps thinly sliced
  1/4 teaspoon kosher or sea salt
  1/4 teaspoon freshly ground black pepper
  1 bulb fennel, thinly sliced, foliage stemmed
  1 can or 1 1/2 cups cooked white beans, drained
  1 can or 6–7 ounces cooked tuna, drained
  12 stalks asparagus, ends snapped
  1 tablespoon lemon juice
  1/4 cup basil, shredded

Cook pasta according to package directions. While water is heating, toast nuts in a dry pan over medium high heat until golden (2–3 minutes), set aside. In a wide, shallow pan, heat oil, garlic, and rosemary over medium high heat for 1 minute, add mushrooms, salt, and pepper and cook for 2 minutes. Add fennel, stir to coat, cover pan and cook, covered until barely tender (3–4 minutes). Stir in beans and tuna, cover pan and bring to a simmer (2–3 minutes). Add asparagus spears, cover and cook until barely tender (2–3 minutes). Toss with hot, drained pasta and lemon juice, garnished with basil and pine nuts. Serves 4.

"Exquisite space and delicious food."

Springtime Salmon Salad

Try this elegant ensemble when you have leftover poached fish of any kind.

2 cups baby spinach
2 cups mixed greens
2 cups bok choy or Napa cabbage, shredded
2 cups arugula or radicchio, shredded
1 cup cucumber, finely chopped
1–2 cups poached or smoked salmon, thinly sliced
4 green onions, thinly sliced
1/4 cup Springtime Ginger Dressing (see below)
1 cup daikon or any sprouts

Gently toss spinach, mixed greens, bok choy, and arugula and divide among four plates. Top each with cucumber, fanned salmon slices, and green onions. Drizzle with dressing and serve, garnished with sprouts. Serves 4.

Springtime Ginger Dressing

Try this lively dressing on mixed greens, baked potatoes, or grilled vegetables.

1/2 cup canola oil
1/3 cup rice vinegar
1–2 teaspoons fresh ginger root, grated
2 tablespoons garlic greens or chives, finely chopped
1/2 teaspoon shoyu or tamari soy sauce

In a jar, combine oil, vinegar, ginger, garlic greens or chives, and soy sauce. Shake well to emulsify. Refrigerate leftovers for up to 3 days. Makes about 1 cup.

"Nicely paced. Excellent facilitation. This was a wonderful day. I feel warm, safe, and at peace."

Cooking at Harmony Hill

Grilled Salmon
with Lavender and Basil

Harmony Hill's meditative lavender labyrinth provides the
kitchen with all the fragrant blossoms we can use. To end up
with leftovers for salads and omelets, double the recipe.

> 1 organic lemon, 1/2 juiced and zest grated,
>   1/2 cut in quarters
> 4 tablespoons fruity olive oil
> 1 tablespoon shoyu or tamari soy sauce
> 1/4 cup large leaf (Genovese type) basil, shredded
> 1 teaspoon fresh or dried lavender
> 4 salmon steaks (about 2 pounds)

Combine lemon juice, zest, olive oil, soy sauce, basil, and
lavender in a large zip-closure bag. Shake well to blend,
add the salmon and gently massage bag to cover fish with
marinade. Let stand for at least 15 minutes or refrigerate for
an hour. Grill or broil fish for 4–6 minutes per side, basting
each side twice with marinade. Serve at once, with a spritz of
lemon. Serves 4–6.

*"Harmony Hill has been so valuable for helping me get through
my cancer experience. I have a chance to emotionally relax
and let others care for me for a while. I feel revived."*

Garlic Shrimp

With most groups, it's best to offer tasteful tidbits that are easy to handle. Serve this one when you are also having corn on the cob, so nobody minds if you have butter dribbling down your chin. Messy? You bet. Tasty? Oh my.

2 pounds easy-peel large shrimp (backs split and deveined)
2 tablespoons virgin olive oil
1 tablespoon butter
4–5 cloves garlic, minced
1/4 teaspoon kosher or sea salt
1/4 teaspoon freshly ground black pepper
1/4 cup fresh Italian parsley, chopped

In a large heavy skillet, heat oil and butter over medium high heat until butter melts. Add garlic and cook for 1 minute. Shake pan to distribute garlic and add shrimp. Cook for 2 minutes, flip shrimp and cook on second side for 2 minutes or until opaque. Sprinkle with salt, pepper, and parsley and serve hot. Serves at least one.

Hot Tuna Salad

Smoked albacore combines delectably with plump blackberries, juicy melon, and fresh chile peppers. Use mild Hungarian Yellow chiles or zippy Jalapenos, according to your taste.

1 tablespoon virgin olive oil
2 cloves garlic, chopped
1 Hungarian Yellow or Jalapeno chile, seeded
    and finely chopped
1/2 cup Walla Walla Sweet onion, chopped
1/4 teaspoon kosher or sea salt
1 cup ripe Casaba or any melon, diced (1/2 inch)
1 cup blackberries or Marionberries
6–8 ounces smoked albacore tuna, thinly sliced,
    or 6–8 ounces tempeh, thinly sliced
1 tablespoon balsamic or cider vinegar
1 teaspoon capers, drained
1/4 cup flat Italian parsley, stemmed

Heat oil with garlic and 1 teaspoon Hungarian Yellow or Jalapeno chile in a heavy skillet over medium high heat. Add onion, sprinkle with salt and cook for 2 minutes. Add melon and blackberries and cook until warm through (2–3 minutes). Add tuna and cook for 1 minute. Add vinegar and capers and heat for 1 minute. Adjust hot pepper to taste. Garnish with parsley and serve. Serves 4.

Peachy Chipotle Prawns

Sweet and spunky, with just enough chipotle to wake up the subtle shadings of flavor in fully ripe peaches. If your peaches are less than perfect, a little fructose awakens fruit flavors without the overpowering sweetness of sugar.

    2 ripe sweet peaches or nectarines
    1 tablespoon virgin olive oil
    1 clove garlic, chopped
    1 organic lime, rind grated, cut in quarters
    35–40 (about 2 pounds) prawns, peeled and deveined
    1/8 teaspoon kosher salt
    1/2 cup Walla Walla Sweet onion, chopped
    1/2 teaspoon fructose or sugar (optional)
    1 4-ounce can chipotle chiles in adobo sauce, pureed

Heat a saucepan with enough water to cover peaches. Bring to a boil over high heat, add peaches and boil for 30 seconds. Drain and peel, set aside. In a heavy frying pan, heat oil with garlic and lime rind over medium high heat for 1 minute. Add prawns, sprinkle with salt and cook for 2 minutes. Turn prawns and cook until opaque (1–2 minutes). Add onion and cook for 2 minutes. Slice peaches and juice directly into the pan, reduce heat to medium low and heat through (3–4 minutes). If peaches are tart rather than sweet, add fructose to taste. Add 1/2 teaspoon chipotle puree, stir well and serve, garnished with lime wedges. Refrigerate remaining chipotle puree in a glass container for up to a month. Serves 4.

Pasta with
Summery Clam Sauce

Ripe tomatoes and tender clams give this simple dish the savor
of summer. If you like, substitute scallops or tiny shrimp and
chop in fresh basil, cilantro, chives, or oregano.

> 8–10 ounces fresh pasta
> 2 teaspoons virgin olive oil
> 2 shallots or 3 garlic cloves, chopped
> 1/2 red onion, thinly sliced
> 1/4 teaspoon kosher or sea salt
> 2 small zucchini, quartered lengthwise
> 1 cup green beans, ends trimmed
> 1 pint shucked clams
> 2 cups ripe tomatoes, chopped (with juices)
> 1/4 teaspoon freshly ground black pepper
> 1 cup sour cream or plain yogurt (lowfat works fine)
> 1/2 cup Parmesan, Romano, or Asiago cheese,
>   coarsely grated

Cook pasta according to package directions and drain (do not
shock with cold water). While pasta water heats, combine oil,
shallots, onion, and salt in a wide, shallow pan over medium
high heat and cook until barely soft (3–5 minutes). Add
zucchini and green beans and cook until barely tender (3–4
minutes). Add clams and cook, stirring, for 2 minutes. Add
tomatoes and pepper, bring to a simmer, stir in sour cream and
serve over hot pasta, garnished with cheese. Serves 4–6.

*"The staff are superb. The location is ideal. Food is wonderful.
Atmosphere is warm and welcoming."*

Scallops with Matsutake Mushrooms

Matsutake or pine mushrooms have firm, succulent stems with the texture of sea scallops. Sliced into buttons, these woodland treasures partner deliciously with scallops, but chanterelles or any favorite mushrooms taste great, too.

   1 cup jasmine rice
   2–3 (about 2 cups) Matsutake mushrooms
   1 teaspoon virgin olive oil
   1 teaspoon butter
   1/2 cup white or yellow onion, chopped
   1 yellow bell pepper, chopped
   1 pound sea scallops, rinsed
   1/8 teaspoon kosher or sea salt
   1/8 teaspoon freshly ground black pepper

Cook rice according to package directions. Brush mushrooms clean. Peel the stems and slice crosswise into buttons 1/4 inch thick. Slice the caps thinly. In a frying pan over medium high heat, combine oil, butter, and mushrooms and cook until barely browned (3–5 minutes). Turn and brown the other side. Add onion and peppers, cover pan and cook until barely tender (2–4 minutes). Add scallops and cook for 3 minutes per side, turning once. Season to taste with salt and pepper and serve over rice. Serves 4.

"The Harmony Hill experience has completely changed my outlook on life and on my need to get back into the world. I have had my internal battery charged and I didn't even know I was on empty!"

Grilled Arctic Char
with Apple Lime Salsa

This quick rub of fresh lime rind and sea salt also offers a lively counterpoint for the rich flavor of tilapia or Pacific halibut.

> 1 1/2 pounds Arctic char fillet
> 1 organic lime, juiced, rind grated
> 1/4 teaspoon kosher or sea salt
> 2–3 cups Apple Lime Salsa (see below)

Rinse char, pat dry, then sprinkle with lime juice. Combine lime rind and salt and rub on skinless side of fish. Grill, skin side down, over medium coals for 10 minutes or until it reaches 136 degrees F. Tent with foil, let stand for 5 minutes. Serve with Apple Lime Salsa. Serves 4–6.

Apple Lime Salsa

This crunchy, bold blend of diced apple, fennel, and red onion is also terrific over halibut, salmon, or chicken.

> 2 Honeycrisp or Pink Lady (or any) apples, cored and diced
> 1 cup fennel bulb, chopped
> 1/4 cup red onion, chopped
> 1/4 cup cilantro, stemmed
> 1 lime, juiced
> 1/4 teaspoon kosher or sea salt
> 1/4 teaspoon chipotle pepper flakes

In a bowl, combine all ingredients, toss gently and let stand at least 15 minutes before serving. Refrigerate leftovers for up to 2 days. Makes about 3 cups.

"What a wonderful opportunity the contributors created to assist the huge percentage of our communities who are learning to live with cancer. We are now more at peace and will be healthier for the remainder of our lives."

Marinated Tilapia with Smoked Tomato Dressing

Intensely flavorful dressings can be overpowering in salads but work beautifully as marinades. Any potent salad dressing, from Thai peanut to lemon garlic, will work wonderfully in this speedy recipe.

> 1 pound skinless tilapia fillet
> 2 tablespoons Smoked Tomato Dressing (see below)
>   or any strong dressing
> 2 tablespoons toasted almonds, chopped

Pour the dressing into a frying pan. Add fish, turning to coat completely. Cover pan and cook over medium heat until opaque (internal temperature of 136 degrees F, about 6–8 minutes). Let stand, covered, for 5 minutes, then serve warm, garnished with toasted almonds. Serves 4.

Smoked Tomato Dressing

Substitute sun-dried tomatoes or roasted mushrooms for a new twist on this great dressing.

> 1/4 cup dried smoked tomatoes, chopped
> 1/4 cup virgin olive oil
> 1 clove garlic, chopped
> 2 teaspoons Grade B maple syrup or honey

Soak tomatoes in hot water to cover until soft (15–20 minutes). Place in a food processor with oil, garlic, and maple syrup and puree to a coarse paste, adding water as needed to achieve desired consistency. Store excess in a tightly sealed glass jar in the refrigerator for up to a week. Makes about 3/4 cup dressing.

"I would say Harmony Hill is true to its name—the setting and the content of retreats promote harmony in this busy world!"

Salmon with Black Bean Sauce and Cilantro

The spicy, Asian-inspired sauce is excellent spooned over hot rice, with a side of fresh local greens.

    2 teaspoons virgin olive oil
    1 shallot, chopped
    2 stalks celery, chopped
    1 pound skinless salmon fillet, cut in 4 pieces
    1–2 tablespoons black bean sauce
    1–2 teaspoons oyster sauce
    1/4 teaspoon soy sauce
    1/4 cup cilantro, stemmed

In a pan, heat oil with shallot and celery over medium high heat for 2 minutes. Add black bean sauce, oyster sauce, and soy sauce, add salmon and turn twice to cover. Cover pan, bring to a simmer, reduce heat to medium low and cook until opaque (10–12 minutes). Remove from heat, let stand 5 minutes, then serve, garnished with cilantro. Serves 4.

Baked Mackerel

A tart masque of yogurt and dill gives mackerel a clean, lean flavor. Bon appetit!

    1 1/4 pounds mackerel fillet
    1 cup plain yogurt (nonfat works fine)
    1 teaspoon dried dill, crumbled
    1/8 teaspoon kosher or sea salt
    1/4 teaspoon smoked paprika

Place fish in a baking dish, skin side down. Combine yogurt, dill, salt and paprika and spoon over fish, covering all exposed skinless, areas, top and sides. Put in a cold oven and bake at 300 degrees F until done (about 40–50 minutes, to an internal temperature of 136 degrees F). Serve hot. Serves 4.

Trout with Red Grapes and Ginger

Any white fish will work beautifully here, as will all kinds of sweet grapes, from Champagne or Muscat to Concord (seed those first, though).

    1 1/3 pounds filleted trout or tilapia
    2 cloves garlic, chopped
    1 tablespoon grated ginger root
    1/4 teaspoon tamari or soy sauce
    1/4 teaspoon freshly ground pepper
    2 teaspoons mint, chopped, plus four sprigs mint
    2 cups red seedless grapes, halved

Place fish in a single layer in a heavy frying pan. Sprinkle with half the garlic, ginger, tamari, and pepper, adding remainder of each to the pan. Add chopped mint and grapes, then add water until the level reaches halfway up the side of the fish pieces (do not cover fish). Bring to a boil over medium high heat, immediately cover pan and remove from heat. Let stand 10 minutes or until fish reaches internal temperature of 136 degrees F (check after 5–7 minutes). Remove fish to four dinner plates, return pan to high and reduce liquid by half (3–4 minutes). Spoon over fish and serve, garnished with remaining mint. Serves 4.

"A huge thank you! The experience was invaluable. I came to Harmony Hill stressed out and anxious about my cancer but am leaving feeling at peace with myself and my health. Harmony Hill is an incredible place for cancer survivors."

6 Chicken or Not

While most meals at Harmony Hill are vegetarian, cancer patients whose doctors recommend they increase their protein intake may find organic poultry helpful. Lean, tender, and free of hormone or pesticide residues, organic poultry offers high-quality protein in an easily digestible form. You may especially enjoy cooking with European-style poultry such as Smart Chickens™; these are organically grown, uncaged birds that have been fed a balanced, nutritious diet and allowed to roam freely.

To a North American palate, European-style poultry tastes remarkable, reminding many of French or Italian dining experiences. Mass-produced chicken, though cheap, is of such poor quality that it is often "improved" with salty water to plump it up and impart flavor. Check labels next time you buy inexpensive chicken; if it says something like "all natural" and also lists as much as 15% "broth" by weight, that's salt water you're paying for!

Many of the recipes gathered here call for boneless, skinless chicken. Breasts are less moist and less flavorful than thighs, which are also far less expensive, but either works fine, as does organic turkey or lean turkey sausage. Any of these recipes can be made with vegetarian and vegan poultry alternatives. Most grocery stores now stock a wide range of faux-poultry, including mycoprotein-based Quorn™ "cutlets," which have a more appealing flavor and texture than many "veggie burgers."

WINTER
Pomegranate Chicken
Chicken Curry with Winter Greens
Manly Meatloaf
Rosy Lemon Chicken
Turkey with Parsnips and Ginger

SPRING
Turkey Burgers Diane
Strawberry Chicken
Spring Chicken with Rhubarb
Ravioli with Turkey and
    Pan-Roasted Asparagus

SUMMER
Country Chicken Noodles with
    Tangy Tomato Basil Sauce
Tangy Tomato Basil Sauce
Sweet Basil Chicken
Chipotle Chicken

FALL
Blueberry Chutney Chicken
Blueberry Lime Chutney
Golden Chicken Corn Pudding
Autumn Apple Chicken
Apple Ginger Sauce
French Chicken with Mushrooms
Skillet Paprika Chicken
Hot and Sour Cranberry Chicken

"I thought I was attending the retreat for my wife, who was taking my cancer very hard. I found that I benefited just as much or maybe even more. I also learned that 'keeping it all in' did not help either one of us. One participant talked about wanting to remove the barriers that build up between partners, when both are afraid to hurt the other by admitting our pain or fear. Here at Harmony Hill, we learned that sharing those painful truths can be incredibly healing and connecting. We feel close again and there are no more secrets."

Pomegranate Chicken

Loaded with antioxidants, a glass of unsweetened pomegranate juice has become a daily habit for some health-conscious folks.

- 4 boneless, skinless chicken breasts
- 1 cup pomegranate juice (unsweetened)
- 1/4 teaspoon sea salt
- 1/4 teaspoon freshly ground black pepper
- 6 small leaves Black Dragon kale, shredded
- 2 cups Napa cabbage, shredded
- 2 cups red cabbage, shredded
- 1/2 cup Jack cheese, diced, or 1/4 cup fresh
      goat cheese, crumbled
- 1/4 cup cilantro, stemmed
- 1/4 cup pomegranate seeds

Arrange chicken pretty side down in a single layer in a wide, shallow pan, add juice and bring to a simmer over medium high heat. Cook for 5 minutes, flip chicken, sprinkle with salt and pepper, reduce heat to medium low and simmer until done (internal temperature of 165 degrees F, about 20 minutes). Top with shredded greens, cover pan and cook for 5 minutes. Add cheese, cover pan and cook for 5 minutes. Serve hot, garnished with cilantro and pomegranate seeds. Serves 4.

Tip To seed a pomegranate quickly, heavily score the skin into eighths and wiggle a knife into the core. Each section will pop open, obligingly spilling its seeds without a big mess.

"I really appreciate how the staff was so flexible in assisting our group, which had some unusual needs. Everything went so smoothly."

Chicken Curry
with Winter Greens

Lightly toasting seeds and spices boosts fragrance and flavor remarkably. Found in many markets these days, garam masala is a rich and complex blend of Indian spices with deeper flavor and less heat than curry powder.

1 pound yellow-skinned potatoes, diced
1/2 teaspoon salt
1 teaspoon canola oil
1 teaspoon turmeric
1 teaspoon cumin seed or ground cumin
1 teaspoon coriander seed
1 teaspoon garam masala or curry powder
1 pound boneless, skinless chicken, in bite-sized pieces,
    or 2 cups firm tofu, diced
1/2 cup red onions, diced
1 Gala or Fuji apple, cored and diced
4 cups spinach
2 cups mustard greens, shredded
2 tablespoons toasted peanuts or cashews

Cook diced potatoes in boiling water with 1/4 teaspoon salt until tender (5–7 minutes). Drain. In a wide, shallow pan, heat oil, turmeric, cumin, coriander seed, and garam masala over medium high heat until fragrant (about 1 minute). Add chicken and cook until white, turning several times (3–4 minutes). Add onions, remaining salt, and apples and cook for 5 minutes. Add drained potatoes and cook until lightly browned (8–10 minutes). Stir in spinach and mustard greens, cover pan and cook until lightly wilted (3–4 minutes). Serve hot, garnished with nuts. Serves 4.

"Harmony Hill is a perfectly peaceful, welcoming sanctuary for the heart and soul. What can I say—it's wonderful. It feels good to eat here!"

Manly Meatloaf

Ridiculously simple, this healthy version of a classic is a real crowd pleaser. It's great hot, even better cold in sandwiches. If you make this with TVP (textured vegetable protein), use 4 cups total and add an Italian seasoning blend to improve the flavor.

> 1 1/4 pounds lean Italian turkey sausage,
> squeezed from casing
> 1 1/4 pounds lean ground turkey
> 1 cup fresh whole grain bread crumbs

Blend all ingredients well and pack into a bread pan. Press down meat at both ends to allow room for juices to collect. Bake at 350 degrees F until done (internal temperature of 170 degrees F, about 50–60 minutes). Let stand 5 minutes, then slice and serve. Serves 8–10.

Rosy Lemon Chicken

A meal in a pan, this delightfully different dish is perfect for busy nights when you want to eat simply but well. The rosy pan juices are thickened with instant mashed potatoes, but please use a "natural" brand that contains just potatoes, butter, and salt with no extra additives; the flavor difference is outstanding!

> 4 boneless, skinless chicken breasts (frozen OK),
> or 4 soy-based Chik Patties®
> 2 tablespoons lemon juice
> 1 10-ounce box frozen spinach, thawed (microwave OK)
> 1 15-ounce can diced fire-roasted tomatoes in juice
> 2/3 cup feta cheese, crumbled
> 3–4 tablespoons instant mashed potato flakes
> (potatoes, butter, salt)

In a wide shallow pan, spread chicken in a single layer, sprinkle with lemon juice and top with spinach. Add tomatoes and juice, sprinkle on feta, cover pan and bring to a boil over medium high heat. Reduce heat to medium low and simmer until chicken reaches internal temperatures of 165 degrees F (25–30 minutes, 40 if frozen). Stir in potato flakes to desired consistency and serve. Serves 4.

Turkey with Parsnips and Ginger

This quick stir fry tastes terrific over whole grains or rice. If you associate parsnips with the taste of old sweat socks, buy them organically grown and prepare to be amazed. Compost-enriched soil gives these wholesome root vegetables a delicious, sweet flavor and pleasing texture as well.

1 teaspoon virgin olive oil
2 leeks, thinly sliced (white and pale green parts only)
2 inches fresh ginger root, finely chopped
16–20 ounces extra lean ground turkey or
     2 cups TVP (textured vegetable protein)
2 cups parsnip, peeled and thinly sliced
4 cups red chard, shredded
4 cups spinach, stemmed and shredded
1 tablespoon fresh parsley, chopped
2 tablespoons plain rice vinegar
1/2 teaspoon shoyu or tamari soy sauce
2 tablespoons roasted sesame seeds

In a wide, shallow pan or wok, heat oil over medium high heat with leeks and ginger and cook, stirring, for 2 minutes. Add crumbled turkey and cook, stirring, until meat turns white (3–5 minutes). Add parsnip and chard and cook, stirring, until vegetables are barely tender (3–4 minutes). Add spinach and parsley and cook, stirring, for 2 minutes. Add rice vinegar, cover pan and simmer over low heat for 10 minutes. Add soy sauce to taste. Garnish with sesame seeds. Serves 4–6.

Turkey Burgers Diane

Slimmed down and sped up, this healthy version of the classic
Steak Diane is a meal in itself. For tender, succulent bird
burgers, handle ground poultry as little as possible.

    4 whole grain burger buns, split and toasted
    16–20 ounces lean ground turkey, or 4 soy-based
        Chik Patties®
    1 tablespoon Worcestershire sauce
    1/2 teaspoon coarsely ground black pepper
    1 teaspoon virgin olive oil
    3 cloves garlic, chopped
    1/2 onion, thinly sliced
    4 mushrooms (any), thinly sliced
    4 lemon wedges (optional)

Place toasted buns on four plates. Cut ground turkey into four
pieces, pat gently to flatten, then spritz the tops with half the
Worcestershire sauce, patting on half the pepper. In a wide,
shallow pan, combine oil and garlic over medium high heat and
cook 1 minute.

Add burgers, peppered side down, spritz tops with remaining
Worcestershire sauce and pepper and cook for 4 minutes. Flip
burgers, cook for 2 minutes to sear. Add onions and mushrooms,
cover pan, reduce heat to medium and cook until mushrooms
are soft (4–5 minutes). Burgers should be cooked through
and reach an internal temperature of 165 degrees F. To serve,
spread buns with onions and mushrooms, add a burger and
spritz with a lemon wedge. Serves 4.

*"Can't thank donors enough. These retreats give us insight
into our lives as survivors and strategies for moving onward."*

Strawberry Chicken

Perfect for a light lunch or brunch, this spring-inspired dish is a hit with those whose appetite needs tempting. The piquant combination of strawberries with basil and pepper is equally delicious in fruity or green salads. If you use tofu, add it with the greens to avoid overcooking.

    1 teaspoon unsalted butter
    1 teaspoon virgin olive oil
    1 teaspoon celery seed
    1/2 cup onion, chopped
    1/4 teaspoon sea salt
    2 cups skinless, boneless chicken, sliced thinly,
        or 12 ounces firm tofu, sliced thinly
    2 cups Napa cabbage, shredded
    2 cups spinach
    1 cup fresh strawberries, stemmed and halved
    1 tablespoons fresh basil, minced
    1/4 teaspoon freshly ground black pepper

In a wide, shallow pan, melt butter in oil over medium high heat. Add celery seed and cook for 1 minute. Add onion and salt and cook until soft (4–6 minutes). Add chicken, stir to coat, cover pan and cook for 10 minutes. Add cabbage and spinach, cover pan and cook for 10 minutes. Meanwhile, combine strawberries, basil, and pepper, set aside. When chicken is ready, serve hot, garnished with strawberries. Serves 4.

Tip To avoid pesticide residues, always choose organic fruit when it will be eaten whole.

"With health care costs so high in such times, it's wonderful to have a place to go that is concerned with your healing instead of your pocketbook!"

Spring Chicken with Rhubarb

Like lemons, rhubarb packs a mighty tang, but its sour quality is mellowed by tangerines or clementines. Don't add sugar too hastily—let the flavor sing! If you use the soy alternative, reduce the cooking time to 15 minutes.

> 2 cups (2 stalks) rhubarb, in 1/4-inch slices
> 2 organic tangerines or clementines (unpeeled),
>   chopped and seeded
> 2 tablespoons sugar
> 2 teaspoons virgin olive oil
> 2 shallots, chopped
> 1 teaspoon rosemary, chopped
> 1 onion, chopped
> 1/4 teaspoon sea salt
> 2 cups skinless, boneless chicken, chopped,
>   or 4 soy-based Chik Patties®, chopped
> 4 green onions, sliced
> 2–3 tablespoons fresh goat cheese, crumbled

In a food processor, process rhubarb, tangerines, and 1 tablespoon sugar for 30 seconds, set aside. In a wide, shallow pan, heat oil, shallot, and rosemary over medium high heat for 1 minute. Add onions, sprinkle with salt and cook for 5 minutes. Add chicken and cook, stirring for 5 minutes. Add rhubarb mixture, cover pan and cook until chicken is tender (15–20 minutes). Season to taste with additional sugar and serve, garnished with green onions and goat cheese. Serves 4.

"Hearing everyone else's stories, during the course of the retreat, helped me realize that everyone in the room felt like I did. Hearing my own story come out of someone else's mouth felt surprisingly healing. It meant that none of us need be alone in this experience."

Cooking at Harmony Hill

Ravioli with Turkey and Pan-Roasted Asparagus

Add pan-roasted asparagus to chicken, tuna, or egg salads for a warm, earthy note. To make the tofu version of this recipe, add tofu with carrots to avoid overcooking.

8–12 ounces spinach ravioli
1/4 teaspoon kosher or sea salt
12 spears asparagus, ends trimmed, cut in 1-inch pieces
2 teaspoons virgin olive oil
1 pound ground lean turkey, crumbled,
    or 12 ounces medium tofu, crumbled
1/2 cup red onion, chopped
1 cup carrots, peeled and grated
1 cup dry white wine or broth
4 cups spinach
2 tablespoons dried tart cherries or raisins
1 cup ricotta (nonfat works fine)
2 tablespoons roasted almonds, chopped

Cook ravioli according to package directions, drain and divide among four soup bowls. While ravioli water heats, sprinkle salt in a wide, shallow (dry) pan over medium high heat. Add asparagus and cook, stirring occasionally, until slightly charred (3–5 minutes), set aside. Add oil to salt, crumble in turkey and cook for 5 minutes, stirring. Add onion and carrots, cover pan and cook for 5 minutes. Add wine, bring to a simmer, add spinach and cherries and cook until wilted (3–5 minutes). Stir in ricotta and serve over ravioli, garnished with nuts. Serves 4.

"As a caregiver for my first wife, whose cancer took her away from us too soon, I can understand some of what caring for me must be like for my new wife. The programs for caregivers gave us both relief from the isolation and helped us see ourselves as part of a community."

Country Chicken Noodles with Tangy Tomato Basil Sauce

Braising chicken and vegetables in their own juices makes for a lush, full-flavored dish. Watch them closely though, and add a little water if necessary.

12 ounces fresh noodles or any pasta
2 teaspoons unsalted butter
2 teaspoons virgin olive oil
1 onion, thinly sliced
1/4 teaspoon kosher or sea salt
2 cups skinless, boneless chicken, chopped,
     or 12 ounces firm tofu, diced
1 cup red cabbage, shredded
1 cup shell beans, finely chopped
2 ears sweet corn, kernels cut from cob
2 cups fresh tomatoes, diced with juice
1 cup sweet red peppers, chopped
1 cup sweet yellow peppers, chopped
4 cups spinach, stemmed
1 batch Tangy Tomato Basil Sauce (see next page)

Cook pasta according to package directions. While pasta water heats, melt butter in oil over medium high heat in a wide, shallow pan. Add onion, sprinkle with salt and cook until golden (6–8 minutes). Add chicken, stir to coat, cover pan and cook for 5 minutes. Add cabbage, shell beans, and 1 tablespoon water and cook, covered for 15 minutes. Add remaining vegetables, cover and barely heat through (6–8 minutes). Stir in sauce, cook for 2 minutes and serve over hot, drained pasta. Serves 4.

"The three-day retreat at Harmony Hill turned the maze of cancer into a labyrinth where you can't get lost and there is no wrong turn. The program helped us find a renewed sense of well-being as a couple."

Tangy Tomato Basil Sauce

Toss this garden fresh, uncooked sauce with hot rice, spaghetti, or bowtie pasta.

2 cups fresh tomatoes, diced, with juice
1/4 cup Walla Walla Sweet onion, chopped
1 cup fresh basil, stemmed and shredded
2 tablespoons Parmesan or Romano cheese, grated
1/3 cup virgin olive oil
2 tablespoons balsamic vinegar

Combine all ingredients in a blender or food processor and puree to a coarse paste (5–10 seconds). Makes about 2 cups.

Sweet Basil Chicken

For fullest flavor, use the small-leaved basil beloved of Italian cooks. If you use peaches rather than nectarines, parboil them for 30 seconds and slip off skin before slicing.

1 teaspoon virgin olive oil
2 cloves garlic, chopped
1 organic lemon, juiced, rind grated
2 ripe nectarines, sliced
1 onion, sliced
1/4 teaspoon kosher or sea salt
1/4 teaspoon freshly ground black pepper
2 cups boneless, skinless chicken, sliced in 1/2 inch strips,
    or 4 Quorn™ fillets, sliced
1 cup fresh basil, shredded
2 tablespoons pine nuts, toasted

In a wide, shallow pan, heat oil, garlic, and lemon rind over medium high heat for 2 minutes. Add nectarines and onion, sprinkle with salt and pepper, reduce heat to medium and cook until onions and nectarines caramelize slightly (10–15 minutes). Stir in chicken, lemon juice, and half the basil, cover pan and cook over medium heat until chicken reaches internal temperature of 180 degrees F (12–15 minutes). Serve hot, garnished with pine nuts and remaining basil. Serves 4.

Chipotle Chicken

Chipotle peppers lend subtle, smoky heat to the chicken, while fresh vegetables contribute their essences to the creamy sauce, which tastes like summer in the Southwest.

    4 boneless, skinless chicken breasts (frozen works fine)
    2 cloves garlic, chopped
    1/2 teaspoon kosher or sea salt
    1/2 teaspoon chipotle pepper flakes
    2 red or orange bell peppers, sliced
    2 cups green beans, ends trimmed
    2 ears sweet corn, kernels cut from cob,
        or 2 cups corn kernels (thawed if frozen)
    1 cup sour cream or quark (nonfat works fine)
    1/4 cup cilantro, stemmed

Place chicken in a large, shallow pan and sprinkle with half the garlic, salt, and pepper flakes, then add remainder to the pan. Add water to barely cover chicken (start with 1 cup), cover pan and bring to a boil over medium high heat. Immediately reduce heat to low and simmer until chicken reaches internal temperature of 165 degrees F (10–15 minutes if fresh, 15–20 minutes if frozen). Add peppers, green beans, and corn, cover pan and cook 1 minute. Remove pan from heat and let stand, covered, for 5 minutes, then remove chicken and vegetables to four dinner plates with a slotted spoon. Over high heat, reduce poaching liquid by half and stir in sour cream. Spoon over chicken and serve, garnished with cilantro. Serves 4.

"Although I've had a lot of support from friends and family, it is not as uplifting as talking with other women who've been through or are going through this experience. I live in a small town, so this is the first really healing group experience I've had since my diagnosis six months ago."

Blueberry Chutney Chicken

Fresh blueberry chutney gives grilled chicken a summery twist. Chicken on the bone is far tastier when grilled than skinless, boneless pieces, but either kind will work.

> 4 chicken breasts, with skin and bones
> 2 limes, juiced, or 1/4 cup lime juice
> Blueberry Lime Chutney (see below)

Preheat grill or start coals. Marinate chicken in lime juice for at least 15 minutes. Cook on grill for 10–15 minutes per side, flipping once (to internal temperature of 165 degrees F). Remove to serving platter, tent loosely with foil, and let stand for 10 minutes. Serve with Blueberry Lime Chutney. Serves 4.

Blueberry Lime Chutney

Try this sassy fresh chutney with chicken or grilled fish.

> 1 organic lime, juiced, rind grated
> 2 cloves garlic, minced or pressed
> 1 cup fresh blueberries, stemmed
> 1/4 cup Walla Walla Sweet onion, finely chopped
> 1 Ancho or Jalapeno chile, seeded, finely chopped
>   (wear gloves)
> 1/2 teaspoon cinnamon
> 1/2 cup cilantro, stemmed

In a bowl, combine all ingredients, stir well and let stand at least 15 minutes. Serve at room temperature. Serves 4.

"After being here, at Harmony Hill, I am no longer alone."

Golden Chicken Corn Pudding

Comforting and delicious, this is a terrific way to transform leftover poultry into a ravishing new dish.

> 1 teaspoon virgin olive oil
> 2 cups cooked chicken, in bite-sized pieces,
>   or 4 soy-based Chik Patties®, chopped
> 3 ears sweet corn, kernels trimmed,
>   or 3 cups whole kernel corn
> 1 cup half-and-half or milk (nonfat works fine)
> 2 large eggs, lightly beaten
> 1/4 cup cilantro, stemmed and shredded
> 2 green chiles, seeded and chopped (wear gloves),
>   or 1 can (4–6-ounces) green chiles, chopped
> 1 tablespoon flour
> 1/4 teaspoon salt
> 1/4 teaspoon oregano

Preheat oven to 350 degrees F. Oil a baking dish with olive oil, layer on chicken, set aside. In a blender or food processor, combine half the corn with the milk and process to a coarse puree. In a bowl, combine pureed corn, whole corn, eggs, cilantro, 1/4 cup green chiles, flour, salt, and oregano and stir to blend. Pour over chicken in baking dish and bake at 350 until golden (30–40 minutes). Serves 4–6.

"We felt so cared for as a couple. There was so much support for me as a man with cancer and for my wife as a woman trying to support me through this chaotic and uncertain time. We both came away with powerful new tools we still use."

Autumn Apple Chicken

Cider-poached chicken is spicy with cinnamon and a gingery fresh apple sauce.

> 4 skinless, boneless chicken breasts, or
> > 4 faux-chicken fillets
> 1/4 teaspoon sea salt
> 1/4 teaspoon freshly ground black pepper
> 1/2 teaspoon cinnamon
> 1 cup fresh cider (unsweetened)
> 1 cup Apple Ginger Sauce (see below)

Arrange chicken in a wide, shallow pan, sprinkle with salt, pepper, and cinnamon. Add cider to not quite cover chicken (you may not need it all) and bring to a simmer over medium high heat. Cover pan, reduce heat to medium low and simmer until chicken is done (internal temperature of 165 degrees F, about 20 minutes or so). Serve hot with Apple Ginger Sauce. Serves 4.

Apple Ginger Sauce

Not your average apple sauce, this is also great over grilled fish and makes a lively tuna salad for sandwiches.

> 1 cup plain yogurt (nonfat works fine)
> 2 tablespoons mayonnaise
> 1 Honeycrisp or Fuji apple, cored and chopped
> 1 tablespoon fresh ginger, peeled and finely chopped
> 1 clove garlic, minced or pressed
> 1 teaspoon mint, stemmed and chopped
> 1/8 teaspoon kosher or sea salt
> 1/4 teaspoon freshly ground black pepper
> 1 tablespoon cider vinegar

Combine all ingredients in a food processor or blender and process for 5–10 seconds. Makes about 2 cups.

"My life had stopped. Now I can begin living again in a whole new way."

French Chicken with Mushrooms

Simple yet sophisticated, this is French comfort food at its best, especially made with local chanterelles.

    2 teaspoons each virgin olive oil and butter
    2 shallots, chopped
    1/4 cup onion, finely chopped
    1/4 cup carrot, finely chopped
    1/4 cup celery, finely chopped
    1 teaspoon fresh thyme, stemmed and chopped
    1/4 teaspoon sea salt
    1/4 teaspoon freshly ground black pepper
    4 skinless, boneless chicken breasts or 4 Quorn™ fillets
    1/2 cup dry white wine or broth
    1/2 pound chanterelles, Crimini or any mushrooms, sliced
    1 teaspoon capers, drained (optional)
    2 tablespoons flat Italian parsley, chopped

In a wide, shallow pan, heat oil and butter over medium high heat with shallots. Cook 3 minutes, then add onion, carrot, and celery, sprinkle with thyme and half the salt and pepper and cook until soft (3–5 minutes). Add chicken and wine, cover pan and cook until almost done (internal temperature of 165 degrees F, 15–20 minutes). Cover with mushrooms, sprinkle with remaining salt and pepper and capers, cover pan and simmer over medium low heat for 10 minutes. Let stand for 5 minutes, then serve, garnished with parsley. Serves 4.

Skillet Paprika Chicken

Smoked paprika adds depth to any dish and makes fast-cooking entrees like this one taste like they simmered all day.

    2 teaspoons virgin olive oil
    3 cloves garlic, chopped
    3 cups boneless, skinless chicken, chopped, or 4 soy-based
        Chik Patties®, chopped
    1 large onion, chopped
    1/4 teaspoon kosher or sea salt
    2 teaspoons smoked paprika

2 cups yellow-skinned potatoes, chopped
1 yellow bell pepper, thinly sliced
2 cups Crimini or any mushrooms, thinly sliced
1/4 cup heavy cream or sour cream (nonfat works fine)

In a wide, shallow skillet, combine oil, garlic, chicken, onion, salt, and paprika over medium high heat and cook until chicken is lightly browned (3–5 minutes). Add potatoes, stir to coat, cover pan and cook for 3 minutes. Add 2 tablespoons water, cover pan, reduce heat to medium and simmer for 20 minutes. Layer on peppers and mushrooms (do not stir in), cover pan and cook for 10 minutes. Pour in cream, heat through and serve. Serves 4–6.

Hot and Sour Cranberry Chicken

Grade B maple syrup is darker in color and deeper in flavor than costlier Grade A syrup. It offers the perfect counterpoint to sassy cranberries and savory chicken.

1 teaspoon virgin olive oil
4 cloves garlic, chopped
2 inches fresh ginger root, peeled and chopped
1/2 teaspoon salt
1 cup fresh cranberries, stemmed
1 quart chicken or vegetable broth
1 cup brown rice or wild rice
1 pound skinless, boneless chicken, thinly sliced,
        or 12 ounces firm tofu, sliced
1 tablespoon Grade B maple syrup
4 baby bok choy, shredded
1 bunch cilantro, stemmed

In a soup pot, heat oil, garlic, ginger, and salt over medium high heat and cook, stirring often, until garlic turns golden. Add cranberries, cover pan, reduce heat to medium and let cranberries pop (about 2 minutes). Add broth, bring to a simmer, add rice, chicken, and maple syrup and simmer until rice is almost tender (about 40 minutes). Add bok choy, cook for 5 minutes, then serve, garnished with cilantro. Serves 4.

7 Seasonal Side Dishes

Many guests are amazed at the variety of vegetables the Harmony Hill kitchen produces each day. Thanks to recent research on plant foods in the human diet, government nutritionists now recommend up to nine daily servings of plant-based foods. Since many of the most popular meals at Harmony Hill include numerous kinds of vegetables in a single dish, we can offer some proven recipes to help you towards this goal.

It helps to remember that variety is as much the point as volume. Each kind and color of vegetable offers a unique blend of nutrients, as well as specific phytonutrients that promote health and battle cancer and other diseases. To expand your repertoire, combine several kinds of vegetables in each side dish.

As a rule, sides will be most successful when they feature two or at the most three main ingredients. For instance, add red bell peppers and sweet onions to corn, or serve zucchini spears with garlic and tomatoes. Many classic sides start with one or more of the aromatic vegetables from the allium clan—onions, garlic, shallots, leeks, and green onions sautéed in a little olive oil. Those who can't eat onions can substitute hot or sweet peppers or smoked paprika, which lends a surprising quality of body to vegetarian dishes.

WINTER

Harmony Hill Hot Slaw
Winter Greens with
    Blood Oranges
Festive Holiday Cabbage
Blissful Baked Potatoes
Spicy Winter Greens with Pears
Baked Sweet Potatoes with
    Pomegranate Dressing
Pomegranate Dressing
Grilled Teriyaki Eggplant
Zesty Asparagus
Brussels Sprouts with Orange
    Herb Dressing
Orange Herb Dressing
Gingered Brussels Sprouts
Romanesco Broccoli
Shredded Beets
Chipotle Cauliflower
Broccoli with Sorrel Sauce
Sorrel Sauce

SPRING

Dandelion Greens
Nettle Greens
Artichokes with
    Wasabi Mayonnaise
Wasabi Mayonnaise
Red Rice with Spring Greens
Asparagus with Shallots and
    Honey Tangerines
Black Tuscan Kale with
    Yellow Peppers
Spring Peas

SUMMER

Cucumbers with Blueberries
Santa Fe Corn
Country-Style Wax Beans
Italian Zucchini
Sizzling Sesame Squash
Margarita Corn
Tomato Salad with Tomato
    Basil Pesto
Tomato Basil Pesto
Shell Beans with Garlic
    Basil Sauce
Pepper Corn

FALL

Roasted Cauliflower and Brocco-
    flower with Cherry Tomatoes
Brussels Slaw
Magnificent Mushrooms
Creamy Chanterelles
Autumn Cabbage with Gorgonzola
    and Walnuts
Caramel Parsnips
Baked Winter Roots with
    Pumpkin Vinaigrette
Harmony Hill Pumpkin Vinaigrette
Orange Garlic Rice
Lovely Leeks
Wasabi Millet
Cauliflower with Fresh
    Lemon Dressing
Fresh Lemon Dressing
Purple Cauliflower with
    Rainbow Carrots
Spicy Roasted Sweet Potatoes

Harmony Hill Hot Slaw

Of all natural, whole foods, cabbage evokes the highest anti-cancer response in the human body. This protective vegetable offers plentiful antioxidants as well as vitamins and minerals, making it an excellent choice for frequent use for all of us.

> 2 teaspoons canola oil
> 1 teaspoon caraway or celery seed
> 1 onion, chopped
> 1 green pepper, seeded and chopped
> 1/4 teaspoon kosher or sea salt
> 2 cups red cabbage, very thinly sliced
> 2 cups Savoy cabbage, shredded
> 1 sweet apple (Fuji, Gala, or Pink Lady),
>   cored and diced
> 2 tablespoons balsamic or cider vinegar
> 1/4 teaspoon freshly ground black pepper
> 1 cup sour cream (nonfat works fine)

In a wide, shallow pan, heat oil and caraway or celery seed over medium high heat for 1 minute. Add onion, green pepper, and salt and cook until barely soft (2–3 minutes). Add cabbages and apple, stir to coat, cook for 2 minutes. Add vinegar and pepper, cover pan and cook until barely tender (4–6 minutes). Stir in sour cream and serve. Serves 4.

Winter Greens
with Blood Oranges

Winter brings ruby-stained blood oranges to the market. Exquisite juiced, these phytonutrient-rich gems are also delightful in salads and stir fries. To peel them fast, slice off the outer rind and chop the inner sections.

2 teaspoons virgin olive oil
2 cloves garlic, chopped
2 leeks, thinly sliced (white and palest green parts only)
2 blood oranges, peeled and chopped
2 cups kale, stemmed and shredded
2 cups chard, stemmed and shredded
1/4 teaspoon kosher or sea salt

In a large pan, heat oil, garlic, and leeks over medium high heat and cook, stirring, until barely soft (5–6 minutes). Add oranges, kale, and chard, sprinkle with salt, cover pan and steam until barely tender (2–3 minutes). Serve hot. Serves 4.

Festive Holiday Cabbage

Raw or cooked, cabbage and all kinds of greens are highly nutritious, containing a multitude of phytonutrients that promote health and help combat a remarkable range of human disorders, from cancer to poor eyesight.

1 cup red cabbage, coarsely grated
1 cup green cabbage, coarsely grated
1 red Rainbow carrot, coarsely grated
1 red bell pepper, seeded and chopped
2 tangerines, juiced
1/8 teaspoon sea salt
1/8 teaspoon freshly ground black pepper

Combine all ingredients and serve at room temperature. Serves 4–6.

"A beautiful place for healing and reconnecting to nature and soul. Lovely accommodations, fabulous foods, beautiful grounds. Attentive, warm staff."

Blissful Baked Potatoes

Always use organic potatoes when you intend to eat the crispy skin. You'll be pleasantly surprised at the difference in both flavor and quality.

> 2 large organic baking potatoes
> 1/2 cup ricotta cheese (lowfat works fine)
> 1/2 cup fresh mozzarella cheese (lowfat works fine)
> 1/4 teaspoon freshly ground black pepper
> 1/4 teaspoon kosher or sea salt
> 1/4 cup feta cheese, crumbled
> 1/4 teaspoon smoked paprika or cayenne

Bake potatoes at 350 degrees F until done (about 1 hour). Slice in half lengthwise, scoop potato into a bowl, combine with ricotta, mozzarella, pepper, salt, and feta. Refill potato jackets, sprinkle with paprika, place in a baking pan and bake at 350 until puffed and golden (10–15 minutes). Serves 4.

Spicy Winter Greens with Pears

Spicy and sweet-hot, this succulent side is especially good spooned over rice, millet, or quinoa, or served with baked chicken or fish.

> 1 teaspoon virgin olive oil
> 2 cloves garlic, chopped
> 1/4 teaspoon chipotle pepper flakes
> 1/8 teaspoon cinnamon
> 2 firm red pears, peeled, cored, and diced
> 1 leek, thinly sliced (white and palest green parts only)
> 2 cups bok choy, stemmed and shredded
> 2 cups chard, stemmed and shredded
> 1 cup Savoy cabbage, finely shredded
> 1/4 teaspoon kosher or sea salt

In a large pan, heat oil, garlic, chipotle flakes, cinnamon, pears, and leeks over medium high heat and cook, stirring, until barely soft (5–6 minutes). Add bok choy, chard, and cabbage, sprinkle with salt, cover pan and cook until barely wilted (4–5 minutes). Serve hot. Serves 4.

Baked Sweet Potatoes with Pomegranate Dressing

If you use larger sweet potatoes, this sensual side can be a light brunch or evening meal in itself.

    4 medium sweet potatoes
    1 cup sour cream or yogurt (nonfat works fine)
    Pomegranate Dressing (see below)

Prick sweet potatoes with a fork, place in a baking dish and bake at 350 degrees F until tender (30–40 minutes). Slice each open to make a pocket, spoon on sour cream and Pomegranate dressing. Serves 4.

Pomegranate Dressing

Pretty on greens or chopped fruit, this rosy dressing is also great with rice or baked potatoes.

    1/3 cup canola oil
    1 clove garlic, minced
    1 pomegranate, seeded, or 2/3 cup pomegranate seeds
    1 organic lime, juiced, rind grated
    1/4 teaspoon shoyu or soy sauce

Combine all ingredients and stir well. Refrigerate leftovers for up to 3 days. Makes about 2/3 cup.

"This has been an extremely worthwhile experience. I wish it were available to every cancer patient."

Grilled Teriyaki Eggplant

A fat-free eggplant recipe! Grill a few extra slices for crusty sandwiches with wasabi mayonnaise and daikon sprouts. Choose smaller, firm, and glossy eggplants; these youngsters have fewer seeds. Though somewhat lumpy, Sicilian eggplants have the mildest flavor.

     2 medium eggplants, cut in 1/2-inch slices
     1 cup teriyaki sauce or marinade

Preheat the grill. Brush eggplant with sauce on both sides as soon as you slice it and grill over medium heat for 8-10 minutes, turning once. Serve hot. Serves 4–6.

Zesty Asparagus

For a pleasant change, try this with a lime or a satsuma orange.

     16 spears asparagus, ends trimmed
     1 tablespoon virgin olive oil
     3 cloves garlic, peeled and chopped finely
     1 organic tangerine, juiced, rind grated
     1/8 teaspoon kosher or sea salt
     1/8 teaspoon pepper
     1 teaspoon fresh lemon thyme, chopped
     2 tablespoons cilantro, stemmed

Put asparagus in a steamer basket and cook, covered, over medium high heat until bright green and barely tender (3–4 minutes). While they cook, heat oil, garlic, and tangerine rind in a sauce pan over medium high heat to fragrance point (about 1 minute). Add lemon thyme and cooked asparagus, stirring to coat with oil. Sprinkle with salt, tangerine juice, and pepper, cover pan and cook for 1 minute. Serve hot, garnished with cilantro. Serves 4.

"A beautiful place of healing. Calm and quiet, restful. Just what I needed. Food: Delicious. A feast for the eyes as well as the stomach as well as the soul."

Brussels Sprouts
with Orange Herb Dressing

For finest flavor, choose small, firm, tightly closed Brussels sprouts. For best texture, cook until barely tender and remove from heat at once.

> 2 cups firm, small Brussels sprouts,
> quartered lengthwise
> Orange Herb Dressing (see below)

Place sprouts in a steamer basket and cook, covered, over medium high heat until barely tender (2–3 minutes). Remove from heat immediately, toss gently with Orange Herb Dressing and serve. Serves 4.

Orange Herb Dressing

This makes a wonderful marinade for fish or chicken as well as carrots or leeks.

> 1/4 cup virgin olive oil
> 1 organic orange, juiced, rind grated
> 1 tablespoon sweet rice vinegar
> 1/2 teaspoon honey
> 1 shallot, finely chopped
> 1 teaspoon fresh thyme, minced
> 1 tablespoon fresh Italian parsley, minced
> 1 tablespoon fresh mint, minced
> 1/8 teaspoon kosher salt
> 1/8 teaspoon freshly ground black pepper

In a food processor, combine all ingredients and process for 10 seconds. Makes about 1/2 cup. Refrigerate for up to 3 days.

"The kindness and generosity of Harmony Hill donors have provided me with a renewed spirit and helpful tools to nourish my soul."

Gingered Brussels Sprouts

High in phytonutrients, fresh ginger adds a lovely counterpoint to peppery Brussels sprouts and most other vegetables.

 2 cups firm, small Brussels sprouts
 1 tablespoon canola oil
 1 clove garlic, chopped
 1 inch ginger root, peeled and finely chopped
 4 green onions, thinly sliced
 1/4 teaspoon kosher salt
 1 tablespoon toasted sesame seeds

Place Brussels sprouts in a steamer basket and cook over medium high heat, covered, until bright green and barely tender (4–6 minutes). Remove from heat, set aside.

In a wide, shallow pan, heat oil, garlic, and ginger over medium high heat and cook until barely soft (2–3 minutes). Add green onions, sprinkle with salt and cook for 2 minutes. Slice each stemmed sprout in half and add to pan, stirring to coat. Serve at once, sprinkled with sesame seeds. Serves 4.

Tip For optimum health, lighten calorie-dense vegetables such as corn, beans, parsnips, or peas with garlic, onions, celery, and leafy greens. For the biggest nutrient boost, add colorful peppers or Rainbow carrots in red, yellow, orange, white, or purple. Leafy greens are especially nutrient-rich, so aim to add one cup of leafy greens per person (by the time the leafy vegetables cook down, you can end up with just a tablespoon each). If your family is vegetable-averse, puree greens and veggies and sneak them into everything from soups and stews to pasta sauce and meatloaf.

"There are no words to describe the thankfulness I feel for this program, to be able to come to this with my sister is a gift. Harmony Hill has changed our lives in so many ways that will last a lifetime, while cancer itself may not."

Romanesco Broccoli

With its swirling, turret-like spears, Romanesco combines the sweet crispness of broccoli with the firm density of cauliflower. Steam whole or snap off spears and saute.

    2 teaspoons butter
    2 teaspoons virgin olive oil
    1 clove garlic, minced or pressed
    1 organic lemon, juiced, rind grated
    1/2 teaspoon rosemary, stemmed and minced
    3 cups Romanesco broccoli florets,
         stem ends trimmed
    1/4 teaspoon sea salt
    1/4 teaspoon freshly ground pepper
    1 tablespoon flat Italian parsley, stemmed

In a wide, shallow pan, melt butter in oil over medium high heat. Add garlic, lemon rind, and rosemary and cook to fragrance point (about 1 minute). Add broccoli, sprinkle with salt and pepper and cook for 2 minutes. Add 1 tablespoon lemon juice, cover pan and cook over medium heat until bright green and barely tender. Serve hot, garnished with parsley. Serves 4–6.

Shredded Beets

An old-time recipe from the 1920s, this simple method makes the most of tender young beets.

    2 cups (about 1 pound) young beets, shredded
    1 tablespoon butter
    1 tablespoon cider or wine vinegar
    1/4 teaspoon sea salt
    1/4 teaspoon freshly ground black pepper

Place beets in a frying pan with butter, vinegar, and 1 tablespoon water. Cover pan and bring to a boil over medium high heat, reduce heat to medium low and simmer until tender (5–10 minutes). Season with salt and pepper and serve hot. Serves 4–6.

Chipotle Cauliflower

Whether white, orange, green, or purple, cauliflower offers powerful cancer-fighting phytonutrients a well as a lively, peppery flavor. This humble vegetable gains sophistication with a vivid chipotle sauce.

> 1 head cauliflower, stem trimmed
> 1 teaspoon virgin olive oil
> 2 cloves garlic, chopped
> 1 white or yellow onion, chopped
> 1 teaspoon cumin or celery seed
> 1/4 teaspoon sea salt
> 1/4 teaspoon chipotle pepper flakes
> 1/2 cup cream or sour cream (nonfat works fine)
> 2 green onions, thinly sliced

In a soup pot, place the whole head of cauliflower in a steamer basket. Cover pan and cook until tender (8–20 minutes, depending on maturity). Remove from heat, set aside.

While cauliflower cooks, heat oil, garlic, onion, cumin or celery seed, salt, and chipotle flakes in a wide, shallow pan over medium high heat for 3 minutes. Reduce heat to medium low and cook, stirring occasionally, until onions are lightly caramelized (8–10 minutes). Add cream, heat through (do not boil) and pour over cauliflower. Serve hot, garnished with green onions. Serves 4 as an entrée, 6–8 as a side.

"The whole program was valuable. After each session, I would think this was the best so far and then on to the next activity or meal, I'd think this one is, and so on. The opportunity to be taken in and cared for and nurtured by other women at this time in my life means everything to me. I feel blessed with this experience and am truly grateful."

Broccoli with Sorrel Sauce

Nutritious but dowdy, Plain Jane broccoli tastes best when barely cooked and served with a spunky sauce.

   3 cups broccoli, broken in florets, tough ends trimmed off
   1/4 teaspoon sea salt
   1/4 teaspoon freshly ground black pepper
   Sorrel Sauce (see below)

Place broccoli in a steamer basket in a saucepan over an inch of water. Cover pan and bring to a boil over high heat. Reduce heat to medium high and steam until tender (3–5 minutes). Sprinkle with salt and pepper, toss with Sorrel Sauce and serve hot. Serves 4–6.

Sorrel Sauce

Tart and sour, sorrel adds a lemony note to roasted or steamed vegetables and is delightful with grilled fish.

   1/4 cup virgin olive oil
   1 shallot, finely chopped
   1 organic lime, juiced, rind grated
   2 cups French sorrel, finely shredded
   1/8 teaspoon kosher or sea salt
   2 teaspoons capers, drained

Heat olive oil, shallot, and lime rind in a saucepan over medium high heat and cook, stirring, until soft (3–4 minutes). Add sorrel and salt and cook, covered, until sorrel wilts (2–3 minutes). Stir in capers and lime juice to taste and serve. Makes about 1 cup.

"The physical environment is very nurturing and relaxing. The subtle presence is one of nurturing and renewal, and the staff are great. They meet your expectations and they are not intrusive. I especially appreciate the home-like atmosphere of the cottage and the view is beautiful from there. Creekside is a warm, open, bright atmosphere. It is indeed a privilege to be in your sacred space."

Dandelion Greens

European cooks pick fresh spring greens for spring tonics.
Dandelions, nettles, hop vine shoots, and rocket are all
delicious in this simple recipe.

> 4 cups dandelion leaves, well-rinsed
> 2 teaspoons virgin olive oil
> 1 teaspoon cider or wine vinegar
> 2 green onions, finely chopped
> 1/4 teaspoon sea salt

Place greens in a steamer basket and cook, covered, until limp
(3–4 minutes). Toss with remaining ingredients and serve.
Serves 4.

Nettle Greens

Tender young nettles, along with wild onions or ramps, offered
the first taste of spring for Native Americans as well as early
settlers. Wearing gloves and using scissors, gather when stalks
are about 6 inches tall, the leaves still tinged with purple. If
you still get "stung," an over-the-counter antihistamine will
reduce the pain right away.

> 1 gallon (16 cups) young nettles, well-rinsed
> 1–2 tablespoons virgin olive oil
> 4 green onions, chopped
> 1–2 tablespoons balsamic or cider vinegar
> 1/4 teaspoon sea salt
> 1/4 cup Pecorino or Romano cheese, coarsely grated

Heat 2 cups water in a large pot. When boiling, add nettles and
simmer over medium heat until tender (15–20 minutes). Drain,
toss with oil, onions, vinegar, and salt and serve hot, garnished
with cheese. Serves 4–6.

Artichokes with
Wasabi Mayonnaise

Smooth, buttery artichokes benefit from a contrasting sauce or
lively dip.

> 4 large artichokes
> Wasabi Mayonnaise (see below)

Trim artichoke stems to one inch. Pull off the outermost petals
and cut the prickly tops off each petal, then rinse well inside
and out. Place artichokes in a steamer basket over an inch
of boiling water, cover pan, reduce heat to medium and cook
until tender (35–40 minutes). Serve artichokes warm with dip;
scoop a little dip with stem end of each petal, then gently pull
stem end through your teeth to remove the tender inner pith.
Discard tough remaining petals. Serves 4.

Wasabi Mayonnaise

Creamy, tart, and packing some heat, this simple sauce dresses
up any vegetables, whether raw or cooked.

> 1 cup mayonnaise (non- or lowfat works fine)
> 1 to 4 tablespoons wasabi paste

In a bowl, combine mayonnaise with wasabi paste to taste,
starting with 1 tablespoon. Store leftovers in a tightly sealed
glass jar for up to 2 weeks in the refrigerator. Makes about
1 1/4 cups.

How to eat an artichoke
An artichoke is really a large flower and eating one is not an
intuitively obvious process. What look like leaves are actually
petals, tougher on the outside and increasingly tender on the
inside. The inedible core of the artichoke is called the "choke"
for good reason; don't try to eat the fuzzy base! Scrape the
fibers away with a knife to reveal the tender, bowl-shaped
heart above the base of the stem. Slice it up and enjoy with
remaining dip.

Red Rice with Spring Greens

Whole grain red rice cooks as fast as white rice and brings more fiber and nutrients to the table. It cooks up perfectly in 20 minutes and leftovers make excellent cold salads.

    1 cup red rice
    1/2 teaspoon kosher or sea salt
    1 cup snap peas, chopped
    1/2 cup green onions, thinly sliced
    2 tablespoons flat Italian parsley, stemmed and chopped
    1/2 cup daikon radish sprouts, roots removed

In a rice cooker or a saucepan, combine rice with salt and 1 1/2 cups water, cover and cook until tender (20 minutes). Fluff with a fork, let stand 5 minutes, then toss with peas, green onions, and parsley and serve, garnished with radish sprouts. Serves 4.

Asparagus with Shallots and Honey Tangerines

Tangy Honey tangerines, mild rice vinegar, and lively capers balance the natural sweetness of spring asparagus.

    2 tablespoons virgin olive oil
    2 shallots, finely chopped
    20 spears asparagus, ends snapped
    2 Honey tangerines, sectioned, membrane removed
    1/8 teaspoon salt
    1/4 teaspoon freshly ground black pepper
    1 tablespoon rice vinegar
    1 teaspoon capers, drained

Heat oil and shallots in a heavy, shallow pan over medium high heat until shallots release their fragrance and turn pale golden (2–3 minutes). Add asparagus and tangerine sections, sprinkle with salt and pepper and cook until barely tender (2–3 minutes). Add vinegar and capers, cover pan, cook for 1 minute. Toss gently and serve. Serves 4.

Black Tuscan Kale with Yellow Peppers

If you've never willingly eaten kale, you may find that Black Tuscan kale tastes truly good. A cross between kale and cabbage, it's beautiful as an ornamental and its dusky, crinkled leaves are delicious in salads, stir-fries, soups, and omelets.

2 teaspoons virgin olive oil
1 teaspoon fennel or celery seed
2 shallots, chopped
4 cups Black Tuscan kale, stemmed and shredded
1 yellow bell pepper, thinly sliced

In a wide, shallow pan, heat oil, seeds, and shallots over medium high heat for 1 minute. Add kale, then stir to coat, cover pan and cook until tender-crisp (5–6 minutes). Stir in peppers, cover pan and heat through (1–2 minutes). Serve hot. Serves 4.

Tip To shred kale or cabbage, remove the thick stems and cut each leaf in half lengthwise. Stack them together and slice very thinly to make fine ribbons (this is also called a chiffonade).

Spring Peas

The first peas of the season make this classic French recipe truly memorable.

1 tablespoon butter
2 pounds peas, shelled
3 leaves lettuce, rinsed (still wet)
1/4 teaspoon sea salt
1/4 teaspoon freshly ground white or black pepper

Place butter and peas in a saucepan and cover with damp lettuce. Cover pan and cook over low heat until tender (10–12 minutes). Discard lettuce and season peas to taste with salt and pepper. Serve hot. Serves 4.

Cucumbers with Blueberries

This unusual combination is synergistic; each ingredient gains impact from its companions. Use more or less chile pepper, depending on personal preference.

    1 English cucumber, thinly sliced (about 2 cups)
    2 cups blueberries, rinsed
    1/4 cup Walla Walla Sweet onion, chopped
    1/8 teaspoon sea salt
    1 tablespoon lime juice
    1 Jalapeno or Ancho chile, seeded and minced (use gloves)

Gently toss cucumber, blueberries, onion, salt, and lime juice, then add chile pepper to taste. Serve at room temperature. Serves 4–6.

Santa Fe Corn

The sunny, glowing combination of yellow corn, orange carrot, and red pepper is remarkably pretty on the plate.

    1 teaspoon virgin olive oil
    1 teaspoon butter
    2 shallots, chopped
    1 teaspoon cumin seed
    1 carrot, julienned or coarsely grated
    1 red bell pepper, chopped
    4 cups spinach
    1 cup corn kernels (frozen works fine)
    1/4 teaspoon kosher or sea salt
    1/4 teaspoon freshly ground black pepper

In a wide, shallow pan, cook oil, butter, shallots, and cumin over medium high heat for 2 minutes. Add carrots and cook for 2 minutes. Add peppers and spinach, cover pan and cook for 3 minutes. Stir in corn, sprinkle with salt and pepper, cover pan and heat through (2–3 minutes). Serve hot. Serves 4.

Cooking at Harmony Hill

Country-Style Wax Beans

Yellow wax beans have a lovely texture and a flavor that is enhanced by simple ingredients. This recipe provides a slimmed-down version of the way beans used to be cooked on farms all across the country.

> 1 teaspoon butter
> 1/4 cup onion, chopped
> 2 cups yellow wax beans, ends trimmed, chopped
> 1/4 teaspoon sea salt
> 1/4 teaspoon freshly ground pepper
> 1/2 cup cream or sour cream (nonfat works fine)

In a wide, shallow pan, melt butter with onion over medium high heat and cook until soft (2–3 minutes). Add beans, salt, and pepper, cover pan and cook for 2 minutes. Add 1 tablespoon water, cover pan and cook until brightly colored and tender-crisp (2–3 minutes). Stir in cream, heat through (about 1 minute) and serve hot. Serves 4.

Italian Zucchini

Absolutely simple yet unforgettable, this Italian classic turns plain old zucchini into heavenly fare. If you don't have small, freshly picked zucchini, use another recipe; this one is best with perfect ingredients.

> 2 teaspoons virgin olive oil
> 2 cloves garlic, chopped
> 4 6-inch long zucchini, quartered lengthwise
> 1/4 teaspoon sea salt
> 1/4 teaspoon freshly ground black pepper

In a wide, shallow pan, heat oil and garlic over medium heat. Add zucchini, stir to coat with oil, sprinkle with salt and pepper and cook, shaking pan now and then, until tender (5–6 minutes). Serve hot. Serves 4.

Sizzling Sesame Squash

Even dedicated non-squash eaters will ask for seconds of this hot-sweet side. We like the rich, deep flavor of organic toasted sesame oil, but any kind will do.

> 1 teaspoon toasted sesame oil
> 2 cloves garlic, chopped
> 1 inch ginger root, peeled and finely chopped
> 2 tablespoons sesame seeds
> 1 onion, thinly sliced
> 2 stalks celery, thinly sliced on the diagonal
> 2 cups summer squash, thinly sliced
> 2 cups zucchini, thinly sliced
> 1-2 teaspoons Thai sweet red chilli sauce
> 1/4 teaspoon shoyu or soy sauce

In a wide, shallow pan, cook oil, garlic, ginger and sesame seeds over medium high heat for 2 minutes. Add onion and celery and cook, stirring, for 3 minutes. Add squash and zucchini, cover pan and cook until tender (2–3 minutes). Stir in red chilli sauce and soy sauce and serve hot. Serves 4.

Margarita Corn

Fresh lime and sea salt complement sweet corn to perfection. This simple recipe tastes best when sweet corn is freshly picked and barely cooked.

> 4 ears sweet corn, husked
> 1 lime, quartered
> 1/4 teaspoon sea salt

Fill a soup pot with water, bring to a boil and cook corn until barely tender (2–3 minutes). Drain and serve, spritzed with lime and sprinkled with salt. Serves 4.

"The experience at Harmony Hill provided hope and makes me humble."

Tomato Salad
with Tomato Basil Pesto

Nothing beats the taste of sun-ripened tomatoes, fresh from the garden. Tomatoes with less going for them can be bolstered with a few grains of sugar and salt.

    4 ripe tomatoes, thickly sliced
    1 Walla Walla Sweet onion, thinly sliced
    1/8 teaspoon sea salt
    1/8 teaspoon freshly ground pepper
    Tomato Basil Pesto (see below)

On small salad plates, alternate slices of tomato and onion, lightly sprinkling each slice with salt and pepper. Drizzle with Tomato Basil Pesto and serve at room temperature. Serves 4–6.

Tip Never store fresh tomatoes in the refrigerator. The cold will change the natural sugars to starch, flattening the bright, fresh sweet-tart balance. For extra flavor, briefly grill tomatoes before using in sauces or pestos.

Tomato Basil Pesto

Not all pestos are oil-based; in this super healthy version, fresh tomatoes and herbs are bound together with lemon juice. You can even sneak in some tofu to replace the cheese. Nutritional yeast adds a cheesy, nutty flavor without the fat or calories.

    1 cup fresh tomatoes, chopped
    2/3 cup basil leaves, stemmed and torn
    1/4 cup flat Italian parsley, stemmed
    1 tablespoons flaked nutritional yeast (optional)
    1 tablespoon balsamic or cider vinegar
    1/8 teaspoon sea salt
    1/8 teaspoon freshly ground pepper
    1-2 teaspoons lemon juice

Combine all ingredients in a food processor and process for 10–15 seconds. Makes about 1 1/4 cup.

Shell Beans
with Garlic Basil Sauce

If snap beans grow tough, allow them to ripen, then harvest for fresh shell beans or gather them in fall as dried beans for soups.

    2 cups shell beans
    2 cloves garlic, chopped
    1/2 cup basil, shredded
    1 cup plain yogurt
    1/4 cup mayonnaise
    1/4 teaspoon kosher or sea salt

Place beans in a steamer and cook until tender (5–20 minutes, depending on maturity). Meanwhile, mince together the garlic and basil, then blend with yogurt, mayonnaise, and salt. Toss hot beans with sauce and serve. Serves 4–6.

Pepper Corn

When sweet corn is past its first excellence, try this savory treatment next time you fire up the grill.

    8 ears sweet corn, silk removed, husk left on
    1 can (4–6 ounces) chipotle chiles in adobo sauce

Soak corn for 10 minutes in cool water, drain. Lightly shake off excess water and set corn aside. In a food processor, puree chipotle peppers and sauce. Pull the corn husks down, brush puree lightly over corn (you probably won't use it all), then pull husks back over corn to protect the kernels. Grill 3–4 minutes per side, turning several times. Serve hot as a sizzling side for grilled fish or chicken. Serves 4–8.

Tip Store pureed chipotle peppers in adobo sauce in a glass jar in the refrigerator for up to a month. Add a spoonful to dressings, sauces, soups, and sautés for big, bold hit of heat.

Roasted Cauliflower and Broccoflower with Cherry Tomatoes

Broccoflower looks like a pale green cauliflower and, like all cauliflower cousins, can become bitter if overcooked. Unless you are pan-roasting, which sweetens the flavor, keep cooking times brief and serve these tasty vegetables tender-crisp.

   3 cups Cheddar cauliflower (or any), cut in florets
   3 cups broccoflower, cut in florets
   2 cups tart cherry tomatoes
   2-3 teaspoons virgin olive oil
   1/4 teaspoon kosher or sea salt
   1/4 teaspoon freshly ground black pepper

Toss all ingredients, spread one layer thick in a large baking pan and bake at 350 degrees F until tender (30–40 minutes). Serves 4.

Brussels Slaw

Harvest Brussels sprouts after the first frost, which mellows their peppery bite.

   2 cups Brussels sprouts, shredded
   1/4 cup red onion, finely chopped
   1 stalk celery, finely chopped
   1 tablespoon lime juice
   1/2 cup plain yogurt or sour cream (nonfat works fine)

Toss all ingredients in a bowl and serve. Serves 4.

"When we came to Harmony Hill, we were both dying. Now we are living with cancer and the difference is amazing."

Magnificent Mushrooms

Robust and hearty, this velvety, liltingly lemony side is also satisfying when spooned over rice, millet, or quinoa.

    2 teaspoons virgin olive oil
    2 cloves garlic or 2 shallots, chopped
    1 cup onion, chopped
    1 organic lemon, quartered, rind grated
    2 baby bok choy, finely shredded
    2 large Portobello mushrooms, thinly sliced
    1 zucchini, julienne or coarsely grated
    1/4 teaspoon salt
    1/4 teaspoon freshly ground black pepper
    1 teaspoon capers, drained

In a shallow pan, heat oil, garlic, onion, and lemon rind over medium high heat for 2 minutes. Add bok choy, mushrooms, and zucchini, sprinkle with salt and pepper, cover pan and cook until tender (5–7 minutes). Stir in capers and serve with a wedge of lemon. Serves 4.

Creamy Chanterelles

Splendid with grilled fish, this dish is also delectable over rice or baked potatoes.

    1 teaspoon butter
    1 teaspoon olive oil
    1/2 cup onion, chopped
    1/4 teaspoon sea salt
    2 cups Chanterelle mushrooms, thinly sliced
    1 teaspoon green peppercorns, drained
    1/2 cup sour cream (nonfat works fine)

In a shallow pan, melt butter in oil over medium high heat. Add onion, sprinkle with half the salt and cook until slightly caramelized (5–6 minutes). Add mushrooms, stir to coat, sprinkle with remaining salt, cover pan and cook until tender (5–7 minutes). Stir in green peppercorns and sour cream and serve hot. Serves 4.

Cooking at Harmony Hill

Autumn Cabbage with Gorgonzola and Walnuts

Crunchy with apples and walnuts, this simple side gets rave reviews from guests.

  1 tablespoon virgin olive oil
  1 teaspoon dried basil, crushed
  2 tablespoons walnuts, chopped
  1/4 teaspoon sea salt
  1/2 cup red onion, chopped
  2 cups green cabbage, shredded
  1 Braeburn or Cox apple, cored and diced
  1 tablespoon cider vinegar
  2 tablespoons Gorgonzola, crumbled

In a wide, shallow pan, heat oil, basil, walnuts and half the salt over medium high heat until golden (2–3 minutes). Remove walnuts to a plate, add onions and remaining salt and cook for 2 minutes. Add cabbage and apple, stir and cook for 3 minutes. Add vinegar, cover pan and cook until tender (3–5 minutes). Serve hot, garnished with Gorgonzola and walnuts. Serves 4.

Caramel Parsnips

An easy, old-fashioned dish that's a hit with guests of all ages.

  8 parsnips, well-scrubbed
  2 tablespoons butter
  1/4 cup brown sugar

With a spoon, scrape tender skin off whole parsnips. Boil peeled parsnips for 20 minutes in salted water. Drain and arrange in a baking dish, dot with butter, sprinkle with sugar and bake at 400 degrees F until lightly caramelized (25–30 minutes). Serve hot. Serves 4–6.

Baked Winter Roots
with Pumpkin Vinaigrette

Creamy inside with a delightfully chewy crust, these lightly caramelized root vegetables have a sumptuous flavor.

> 2 parsnips, cut in half lengthwise
> 2 turnips, cut in half lengthwise
> 2 carrots, cut in half lengthwise
> 2 Yukon Gold potatoes, cut in half
> 1 tablespoon virgin olive oil
> 1/4 teaspoon sea salt
> Pumpkin Vinaigrette (see below)

Rub vegetables with oil to coat, arrange cut side down in a baking dish and sprinkle with salt. Bake at 350 degrees F until tender (45–60 minutes). Serve hot, with Pumpkin Vinaigrette.

Harmony Hill Pumpkin Vinaigrette

Autumnal and spicy, this piquant dressing is great with greens or an apple-pear fruit salad.

> 1/2 cup cider vinegar
> 1/2 cup canola oil
> 1/4 cup cooked pumpkin pulp, mashed (canned works fine)
> 2 tablespoons honey
> 1/2 teaspoon cardamom or coriander
> 1/4 teaspoon kosher or sea salt
> 1/4 teaspoon freshly ground black pepper

In a food processor, combine all ingredients and puree until smooth. Makes about 1 1/4 cups. Refrigerate for up to 3 days.

"Most of the time, I feel very alone with this experience. At the doctor's office, which is fine otherwise, there's not a lot of time available. Here, at Harmony Hill, there is space for safety."

Orange Garlic Rice

Scrumptious with grilled fish or baked chicken, this is also terrific in rice salad. This is a breeze in a rice cooker—just assemble everything but the orange juice, cook as usual, add juice to cooked rice and fluff with a fork.

   1 cup jasmine rice
   1 organic orange, juiced, rind grated
   2 cloves garlic, chopped
   1/2 teaspoon kosher or sea salt

In a saucepan, combine rice, orange rind, garlic, and salt. Add water according to package directions (usually about 1 1/2 cups), bring to a boil over high heat, reduce heat to low, cover pan and cook until tender (about 20 minutes). Remove from heat, sprinkle with orange juice, fluff with a fork, cover rice and let stand for 5 minutes. Serves 4.

Lovely Leeks

Leeks gain sweetness as the first frost arrives. Serve this savory-sweet side with baked potatoes, chicken, or seafood.

   1 teaspoon virgin olive oil
   2 cloves garlic
   4 leeks, trimmed, quartered lengthwise
   1 onion, thinly sliced
   1/4 cup fresh apple or pear cider
   1/4 teaspoon soy sauce or Bragg Liquid Aminos
   1/4 teaspoon freshly ground black pepper

In a wide, shallow pan, heat oil, garlic, and leeks over medium high heat for 2 minutes. Add onions and cook until barely soft (2–3 minutes). Add cider, soy sauce, and pepper and cover pan. Bring to a simmer, reduce heat to low and cook until tender (8–10 minutes). Serves 4.

Wasabi Millet

This punchy combo also wakes up mild grains such as brown rice, quinoa, oat groats, and kasha.

1 cup millet
2 cups vegetable or chicken broth
1/4 cup flat Italian parsley, chopped
1/4 cup lemon balm, stemmed and shredded
1 cup basil, stemmed and shredded
2 green onions, thinly sliced
1 teaspoon fresh lemon thyme
1/2 teaspoon wasabi paste
1/3 cup sweet rice vinegar
1/3 cup virgin olive oil
1/2 cup buttermilk

In a saucepan, toast millet over medium high heat until fragrant (2–3 minutes). Add broth, bring to a boil, reduce heat to low, cover pan and cook until tender (about 20 minutes). Remove from heat, fluff with a fork, cover and let stand for 5 minutes. Meanwhile, combine remaining ingredients in a food processor or blender and puree. Toss hot millet with wasabi blend and serve. Serves 4–6.

"For a cancer patient with very limited funds, Harmony Hill has been a blessing. It has given me a safe and secure space to interact, share, and shed my many tears of fear, brokenness, despair, grief, and even anger. There is no other space in my life where I have this. Thank you, God, for Harmony Hill."

Cauliflower with Fresh Lemon Dressing

Relatively low in carbs and high in fiber, the cauliflower clan offers almost 2 grams of protein per cup, for around 20 calories (and almost no fat). So why don't we eat this stuff every day? Mostly because we don't know to cook it well.

> 1 head purple, golden, or any cauliflower, cut in florets
> 1/4 teaspoon kosher or sea salt
> 1/4 teaspoon freshly ground black pepper
> 1/4 cup Fresh Lemon Dressing (see below)

Place cauliflower in a steamer basket over boiling water, sprinkle with salt and pepper, cover pan and cook until barely tender (2–4 minutes). Remove from heat and serve, drizzled with Fresh Lemon Dressing. Serves 4.

Fresh Lemon Dressing

Lively and refreshing, this sparkling sauce brilliantly embraces tossed greens or cooked vegetables.

> 1/2 cup virgin olive oil
> 1 organic lemon, juiced, rind grated
> 1 clove garlic, minced or pressed
> 1/4 teaspoon shoyu or tamari soy sauce

In a bowl or small jar, combine oil, lemon juice and rind, garlic, and soy sauce, and blend well. Makes about 2/3 cup.

"Sacred space is a felt experience from the moment you arrive. Then you meet the staff, eat the food, walk the labyrinths, and go home energized with healing in process."

Purple Cauliflower with Rainbow Carrots

Colorful cauliflowers such as Plum Purple or Golden Cheddar taste mild enough to enjoy fresh, retain their color when cooked, and develop a subtle sweetness when roasted.

    1 teaspoon virgin olive oil
    1 teaspoon butter
    1 shallot, chopped
    1 teaspoon rosemary, minced
    1 each red, yellow, white, and orange Rainbow
        carrots, chopped
    2 cups purple cauliflower, cut in florets
    1/4 teaspoon kosher or sea salt
    1/4 teaspoon freshly ground black pepper
    2-3 teaspoons balsamic vinegar

In a wide, shallow pan, heat oil, butter, shallot, rosemary, and carrots over medium high heat and cook for 2 minutes. Cover pan and cook for 5 minutes, shaking pan now and then. Add cauliflower, sprinkle with salt and pepper, cover pan and cook until barely tender (3–5 minutes). Add balsamic vinegar, toss gently and serve. Serves 4.

"Love, love, love the setting. The peaceful and flowery grounds were unexpected but so appreciated. All the necessities and comforts needed to relax and be creative were there: healthy food/treats, caring staff, candles, smells of food cooking, fresh flowers, shower, etc. Without exception, the staff knew how to let us make Harmony Hill our home."

Spicy Roasted Sweet Potatoes

Spunky with ginger and chile peppers, these lively sweet potatoes are delicious with roast chicken or turkey and rich dressing. If you prefer, mash the skinned potatoes with the gingery sauce, but whole potatoes make an attractive and simple presentation.

>   6 medium sweet potatoes
>   2 tablespoons virgin olive oil
>   2 cloves garlic, chopped
>   1 inch fresh ginger root, chopped
>   1-2 Serrano chiles, seeded and chopped
>   1/8 teaspoon salt
>   3-4 tablespoons balsamic vinegar
>   1 cup sour cream (nonfat works fine)

Preheat oven to 350 degrees F. Place scrubbed whole sweet potatoes in a baking dish and bake until tender (35–40 minutes). In a saucepan over medium high heat, combine oil, garlic, ginger, and chiles and cook until barely tender (3–4 minutes). Stir in salt and balsamic vinegar to taste and simmer over low heat until ready to serve. When tender, split each potato lengthwise, drizzle with vinegar sauce and serve hot, garnished with sour cream. Serves 6.

"Your loving kindness was touching and just what I needed at this time in my life. So many times my body gets treated but not my mind and soul, as this program does. I sincerely hope it can continue for other cancer patients because it is so helpful in so many ways."

8 Wraps, Roll-Ups, and Sandwiches

Today's culture seems to value speed over savoring, even when it comes to our daily food. Family meals are rare and often rushed, while fast food is sadly common. Happily, even when kitchen time is short, nutrition need not fall by the wayside. Here is an assortment of quickly made and portable meals that combine terrific taste with sound nutritional value.

Some of these recipes can be made extremely fast if you have cooked or prepped ingredients on hand. As you read through this chapter, you'll note quite a few recipes where lovely leftovers can cut down on prep time. Indeed, you may want to make a practice of cooking extra beans, grains, chicken, or fish when you have more time.

When you prep vegetables for salads or sides, chop a few extras and pop them in the fridge. These ready-to-use ingredients can then be transformed into delicious wraps or sandwiches for busy days.

The freezer can also be your friend. Freeze extra wraps, roll-ups, or sandwiches to take to school or work. By lunchtime, they will be fresh tasting and ready to eat.

"By the time I got to Harmony Hill, my sense of self as a person had been erased by procedure after procedure of cancer treatments. My sense of dignity was totally gone. I was really struggling. I needed to remember myself, put myself back together. During the program, I started feeling like a person again for the first time in a very long time. There was no pity— that doesn't help us move forward—but a genuine compassion. The whole experience was totally life-changing. The experience of the retreat, and the healing that happened, went so deep that I carry it with me now through my life. It has sustained me through some very hard times since then. I thought cancer was the beginning of the end for me. I discovered through the retreat that this wasn't so. The retreat gave me back my life. I was willing to begin again."

Fish Tacos

Sustainably caught and mild in flavor, Pacific halibut works well with a wide array of seasonings. Pan-poached fillets are tender, succulent, and ready to eat in less than 10 minutes.

>   1 pound Pacific halibut fillet, cut in four pieces
>   1/4 cup lemon juice
>   1 cup plain yogurt (nonfat works fine)
>   4 cups spinach, shredded
>   1 teaspoon cumin
>   1/4 cup salsa
>   3 cups cabbage, finely shredded
>   8 corn tortillas
>   1 lime, cut in wedges

In a shallow pan, arrange fish skin side down, sprinkle with lemon juice, cover pan, bring to a simmer over medium heat and cook until opaque (internal temperature 136 degrees F, 6–8 minutes). In a food processor, combine yogurt, spinach, and cumin and puree. Stir in salsa and cabbage, set aside. In a dry frying pan, heat tortillas over medium high heat. Fill with cabbage and fish and serve with a wedge of lime. Serves 4–6.

Speedy Shrimp Tacos

Simple and quickly assembled, these intriguingly spicy treats taste like you worked much harder than you did!

>   2 cups lettuce, shredded
>   4 corn tortillas
>   1 avocado, sliced
>   6–8 ounces cooked, cleaned shrimp
>   1/2 cup cherry tomatoes, halved
>   1/2 cup salsa

Divide lettuce among tortillas and top with avocado. Gently toss shrimp, tomatoes, and salsa and divide among tacos. Serves 4.

Fish Burgers with Creamy Italian Dressing

When you want totally satisfying comfort food in minutes, this one hits the spot. Ready-to-heat patties are perfect for this.

    4 whole grain burger buns, split and toasted
    1 cup Creamy Italian Dressing (see below)
    4 leaves lettuce
    4 slices ripe tomato
    4 slices red or sweet onion
    1 teaspoon virgin olive oil
    1 shallot or garlic clove, chopped
    4 ready-to-heat fish patties

Place toasted buns on four plates, spread each with dressing, add lettuce, tomato, and onion slices. In a wide, shallow pan, combine oil and shallot or garlic over medium high heat and cook 1 minute. Add fish patties and cook for 2 minutes. Flip and cook for 2 minutes to sear. Cover pan, reduce heat to medium and cook until hot through (4–5 minutes). Place a patty on each bun and serve. Serves 4.

Creamy Italian Dressing

Lovely over baked potatoes or cooked grains, this creamy dressing is also great in potato or pasta salads.

    1 cup plain yogurt or sour cream (nonfat works fine)
    1/4 cup virgin olive oil
    2 tablespoons red wine or cider vinegar
    1 clove garlic, minced or pressed
    1/4 teaspoon dried oregano, crumbled
    1/8 teaspoon sea salt

Combine all ingredients in a food processor or blender and puree for 10–15 seconds. Store leftovers in the refrigerator for up to 5 days. Makes about 1 1/2 cups.

Gorgonzola Quesadillas

Lush with cheese and bright with onions, these quickly made treats are always popular. For variety, use extra sharp cheddar, Pepper Jack, or fresh goat cheese and strips of sweet peppers.

    8 6-inch corn tortillas
    3–4 ounces Gorgonzola cheese, thinly sliced
    1/2 cup red or sweet onion, thinly sliced

Preheat oven to 350 degrees F. On a baking sheet, arrange 4 tortillas and top with cheese. Sprinkle with onion and top with remaining tortillas. Bake at 350 until cheese is partly melted (5–6 minutes), flip quesadillas and cook until cheese is completely melted (2–3 minutes). Cut in quarters and serve. Serves 4.

Pesto Garden Burgers

With a whole grain bun, lettuce, and fresh goat cheese, this fast and simple entree is a hearty meal all by itself. For variety, try tasty Quorn™ "chicken fillet" products or black bean patties.

    4 whole grain burger buns, split and toasted
    1/4 cup pesto
    2–3 ounces fresh goat cheese
    8 leaves lettuce
    1/2 onion, thinly sliced
    1 teaspoon virgin olive oil
    1 clove garlic, chopped
    4 Quorn fillets or garden burgers
    1/4 teaspoon coarsely ground black pepper

Place toasted buns on four plates. Spread one side of bun with pesto and the other with fresh goat cheese, then add lettuce and onion. In a wide, shallow pan, combine oil and garlic over medium high heat and cook 1 minute. Add fillets or patties, sprinkle with pepper and cook for 2 minutes. Flip fillets or burgers and cook for 2 minutes to sear. Cover pan, reduce heat to medium and cook until hot through (2–3 minutes). Place a fillet or burger on each bun and serve. Serves 4.

Pesto Pepper Wraps

Folding wraps so they don't leak is easy, as long as you leave the edges clean. You can roll up or fold your wraps any way you like, but they will be easiest to eat if both ends are tucked in before you make your last turn. If in doubt, have extra napkins on hand.

    4 pesto garlic wraps (or any)
    1/2 cup basil pesto (homemade or store-bought)
    2 teaspoons virgin olive oil
    2 cloves garlic, chopped
    2 red sweet peppers, thinly sliced
    1 Walla Walla Sweet onion, thinly sliced
    1/4 teaspoon sea salt (or any)

Preheat oven to 250 F. Warm wraps in a dry frying pan over medium high heat for 30 seconds each. Spread wraps with pesto to within an inch of the edge, set on plates in warm oven In a frying pan, heat oil and garlic over medium high heat until golden (2–3 minutes). Add pepper and onion and sprinkle with salt. Stir to coat and cook until tender-crisp (2–3 minutes). Spoon peppers and onions into wraps, fold and roll up and serve. Serves 4.

Pizza Wraps

If you don't care for mushrooms, stuff these Pizza Wraps with whatever you prefer, from pepperoni pieces to a medley of thinly sliced vegetables.

    4 tomato wraps (or any)
    1/2 cup pizza sauce (homemade or store-bought)
    8 mushrooms, sliced
    1 cup mozzarella cheese, grated

Preheat oven to broil. Place wraps on cookie sheets and spread to within an inch of edge with pizza sauce. Sprinkle with mushrooms and cheese and broil until bubbly (2–3 minutes). Fold and roll up and serve warm. Serves 4.

Smoked Salmon Pockets

Pack split pita pockets with egg, bean, tempeh, or tuna salad and wrap in foil for picnics and beach parties.

    1/4 cup plain yogurt (nonfat works fine)
    1 teaspoon capers, drained
    1 pita pocket bread, cut in half
    2 cups Napa cabbage, finely shredded
    1/2 red bell pepper, thinly sliced
    4 ounces smoked salmon, flaked

Combine yogurt and capers, set aside. Fill each pita half with shredded cabbage, peppers, and salmon. Drizzle with yogurt and serve. Serves 1–2.

Wasabi Tuna Wraps

These boldly flavorful wraps pack well and remain tidy when you really do need to eat in the car.

    1 can (6–7 ounces) albacore tuna in water,
        drained and flaked
    1/2 cup plain yogurt or quark (lowfat works fine)
    1/2 cup mayonnaise (lowfat works fine)
    1-2 teaspoons wasabi paste
    1/4 teaspoon ponzu or soy sauce
    4 spinach or tomato wraps
    2 cups Romaine or Savoy cabbage, finely shredded
    1/2 cup daikon sprouts, root ends trimmed
    1 cup grape or cherry tomatoes, cut in half

In a bowl, combine tuna, yogurt, mayonnaise, wasabi paste, and ponzu or soy sauce, stir well, set aside. Place wraps on four plates (or pieces of waxed paper for to-go food). Fill the center of each with a generous dollop of tuna salad, adding Romaine, daikon sprouts, and tomatoes. Fold over the top and bottom of each wrap and roll up tightly. Serve at room temperature or chilled. Serves 4.

Shrimp Roll-Up Salad
with Lavender Dressing

For an intriguing twist, roll your salad into cornucopias made with large leaves of Romaine lettuce and Genovese basil.

8 large Romaine lettuce leaves.
8 large leaves of Genovese basil
6–8 ounces cooked, cleaned shrimp
4 cups young greens, stemmed
4 green onions, thinly sliced
Lavender Dressing (see below)
8 cocktail picks

Line each Romaine leaf with a basil leaf, set aside. In a bowl, combine shrimp, young greens, and green onions, drizzle with dressing, toss gently. Stuff each Romaine leaf with dressed greens and roll up lengthwise, leaving top slightly open, securing closure with a cocktail pick. Serves 4.

Lavender Dressing

This fresh lavender dressing has a lilting, lively flavor that complements fish or fowl.

1/4 cup virgin olive oil
1/2 organic lemon, juiced, rind grated
1 teaspoon fresh or 1/2 teaspoon dried lavender florets
1/2 teaspoon lemon thyme, stemmed
1/8 teaspoon salt
1/4 teaspoon honey

In a jar, combine oil, lemon juice and rind, lavender, lemon thyme, salt, and honey. Shake well, set aside. Makes 1 cup.

"Thank you. For many of us, we might not have taken the risk or felt we were worth the additional expense after all that our families have sacrificed in medical costs, lost income, and time. You made peace possible in the midst of chaos."

9 Breads and Muffins

Once you get in the habit of baking, your family will never let you stop. Though many folks find mixes convenient, it's almost as quick to make real muffins and scones and they certainly do taste better. This chapter includes Harmony Hill favorite combinations, from Rosemary Blueberry or Cranberry Pumpkin Seed to Pecan Ginger, Blueberry Lemon, and Oatmeal With Red Currants.

Homemade bread is one of the world's most delightful treats. Although many people are intimidated by the very idea of baking, modern yeasts and flours make bread-making a breeze. Here are some great recipes to get started with, including a no-knead oat bread that smells and tastes divine.

Fresh scones and sweet rolls also smell like heaven and make guests feel delightfully coddled. Both benefit from the addition of tart dried fruit such as currants, cranberries, and sour pie cherries. We also like to add chopped crystallized ginger and minced orange, lemon, lime, or grapefruit peel.

MUFFINS

Pecan Ginger Muffins
Cranberry Pumpkin Seed Muffins
Savory Herb Muffins
Rosemary Blueberry Muffins
Savory Cream of Rye Muffins
Blueberry Lemon Muffins
Oatmeal Muffins with
   Red Currants

QUICK BREADS

Pine Nut Pumpkin Bread
Zesty Orange Banana Bread
Double Corn Bread
Chocolate Hazelnut
   Bread Pudding
Savory Cranberry Walnut
   Bread Pudding
Harmony Hill Zucchini Bread
French Cheese Bread (Gougère)

YEAST BREADS

Anadama Bread
No-Knead Double Oat Bread
Ginger Rye Bread

SWEET BREAKFAST TREATS

Nutty Cherry Cream Scones
Double Date Breakfast Rolls
Ginger Orange Scones

Tip Whenever you include citrus rind in a recipe, it's important to use organic fruit, especially if you are serving children or anyone with a compromised immune system. Conventionally grown citrus fruit rind may contain high amounts of pesticide residues.

Tip Fill fragrant, sweet breakfast rolls with dried dates, figs, mango, or pineapple, plus hazelnuts, walnuts, cashews, and poppy or pumpkin seeds. Flavor them with cinnamon, coriander, cardamom, or nutmeg in many tempting combinations.

Pecan Ginger Muffins

Lively with ginger, these delicious muffins partner well with
soup and salads.

    1 cup whole wheat pastry flour
    1 cup unbleached white flour
    3 teaspoons baking powder
    1/2 teaspoon salt
    3 tablespoons sugar
    2 eggs, beaten
    1/4 cup vegetable oil
    1/4 cup toasted pecans, chopped
    2 tablespoons ginger root, grated or finely chopped
    1 cup milk (nonfat works fine)

Preheat oven to 400 degrees F. Line muffin tins with papers.
In a bowl, sift together flours, baking powder, salt, and sugar.
In a larger bowl, beat eggs with oil to emulsify, then stir in nuts
and ginger. Add milk and gently stir in dry ingredients (do not
overmix). Spoon into muffin cups, filling them 1/2 to 3/4 full.
Bake at 400 until golden brown (16–18 minutes). Serve warm.
Makes 12 muffins.

Cranberry Pumpkin Seed Muffins

Toasted pumpkin seeds add low-carb protein to these crunchy
muffins, which are delightful with fresh goat cheese.

    1 cup whole wheat pastry flour
    1 cup unbleached white flour
    3 teaspoons baking powder
    1/2 teaspoon salt
    3 tablespoons sugar
    1/4 teaspoon nutmeg

2 eggs, beaten
1/4 cup vegetable oil
1 organic orange, juiced, rind grated
1/4 cup dried cranberries
1/4 cup toasted hulled pumpkin seeds
1/2–3/4 cup milk

Preheat oven to 400 degrees F. Line muffin tins with papers. In a bowl, sift together flours, baking powder, salt, sugar, and nutmeg. In a larger bowl, beat eggs with oil to emulsify, then stir in orange juice and rind, cranberries, and pumpkin seeds. Add milk and gently stir in dry ingredients (do not overmix). Spoon into cups, filling them 1/2 to 3/4 full. Bake at 400 until golden brown (16–18 minutes). Serve warm. Makes 12 muffins.

Savory Herb Muffins

Freeze any leftovers to use in stuffing or savory bread pudding.

1 cup whole wheat pastry flour
1 cup unbleached white flour
3 teaspoons baking powder
1/2 teaspoon salt
1 tablespoon sugar
2 eggs, beaten
1/4 cup vegetable oil
2 teaspoons fresh rosemary, stemmed and minced
1 teaspoon dry lemon thyme or any thyme, crumbled
2 cloves garlic, minced or pressed
1 cup milk

Preheat oven to 400 degrees F. Line muffin tins with papers. In a bowl, sift together flours, baking powder, salt, and sugar. In a larger bowl, beat eggs with oil to emulsify, then stir in rosemary, thyme, and garlic. Add milk and gently stir in dry ingredients (do not overmix). Spoon into cups, filling them 1/2 to 3/4 full. Bake at 400 until golden brown (16–18 minutes). Serve warm. Makes 12 muffins.

Rosemary Blueberry Muffins

Fresh or frozen berries work fine in these quickly made muffins.
You can also use blackberries, boysenberries, or Marionberries
with excellent results.

    1 tablespoon virgin olive oil
    1 cup blueberries (frozen work fine)
    2 cups whole wheat pastry flour
    3 teaspoons baking powder
    1/2 teaspoon salt
    1/4 teaspoon freshly ground black pepper
    1 tablespoon sugar
    1 egg, beaten
    1 cup buttermilk or any milk (nonfat works fine)
    2 teaspoons rosemary, stemmed and chopped
    2 teaspoons capers, well drained

Preheat oven to 400 degrees F. Lightly oil a muffin tin or line
with paper cups. Roll blueberries in flour, set aside. In a bowl,
sift together remaining flour, baking powder, salt, pepper, and
sugar. In a larger bowl, blend egg and milk with remaining
oil, rosemary, and capers. Quickly stir dry ingredients into wet
ones (batter will be lumpy). Fold in blueberries and spoon into
muffins cups, filling them 1/2 to 3/4 full. Bake at 400 until set
and golden (15–18 minutes). Makes 12.

*"This retreat was the first time I have been able to talk about
my cancer with others. The three days at Harmony Hill gave
me time to get to know other people and to feel comfortable
enough to talk. Other support groups were too much of an
unknown for me and I did not feel comfortable in them. This
retreat has helped me to focus on the important stuff!"*

Savory Cream of Rye Muffins

Excellent with an omelet or scrambled eggs.

> 1/3 cup canola or virgin olive oil
> 2 cloves garlic, chopped
> 1/3 cup walnut pieces
> 1/2 white or yellow onion, finely chopped
> 1 egg, slightly beaten
> 1 cup buttermilk or yogurt (nonfat works fine)
> 1 cup whole wheat pastry flour
> 1 cup Roman Meal Cream of Rye cereal
> 1/2 teaspoon salt
> 1 tablespoon sugar
> 2 teaspoons baking powder
> 1/2 teaspoon baking soda

Preheat oven to 400 degrees F. Line a muffin tin with paper cups. In a frying pan, heat 1 tablespoon oil and garlic over medium high heat until pale golden. Add the walnuts and cook, stirring, until crisp (3–5 minutes). Set nuts aside on a plate. Add onions to oil and cook, stirring, until soft (3–4 minutes). Remove from heat, set aside.

In a bowl, beat together the egg, buttermilk, and remaining oil. Add onions and garlic, set aside. In a second bowl, blend dry ingredients, then stir quickly into milk mixture. Add nuts, then spoon into muffin cups, filling them 1/2 to 3/4 full. Bake at 400 until puffed and golden (20–25 minutes). Cool on a rack for 5 minutes before serving. Makes 12 muffins.

"In my five years of experiencing three different types of cancer, I've never felt as nurtured as I do at Harmony Hill."

Blueberry Lemon Muffins

By fall, the Harmony Hill freezers are full of plump ripe blueberries. We love the taste of summer they bring to the breakfast table.

> 1 cup whole wheat pastry flour
> 1 cup unbleached white flour
> 3 teaspoons baking powder
> 1/2 teaspoon salt
> 3 tablespoons sugar
> 1 cup blueberries, fresh or frozen
> 2 eggs, beaten
> 1/4 cup vegetable oil
> 1 organic lemon, juiced, rind grated
> 2/3 cup milk (nonfat works fine)

Preheat oven to 400 degrees F. Line muffin tins with papers. In a bowl, sift together flours, baking powder, salt, and sugar. Stir in blueberries to coat with flour mix. In a larger bowl, beat eggs with oil to emulsify, then stir in lemon juice and rind. Add milk and gently stir in dry ingredients (do not overmix). Spoon into cups , filling them 1/2 to 3/4 full, and bake at 400 until golden brown (16–18 minutes) Serve warm. Makes 12 muffins.

"People do care about others. This retreat was a chance to renew trust and faith in the community that extends much tenderness and generosity to reaching out and helping a person become revitalized, hopeful, and able to face the conditions that often keep knocking one down."

Oatmeal Muffins
with Red Currants

Heart-healthy oats work their way into many meals at Harmony Hill. Leftover muffins are wonderful split and toasted.

    1 cup whole wheat pastry flour
    1 cup unbleached white flour
    3 teaspoons baking powder
    1/2 teaspoon salt
    2 tablespoons sugar
    1/2 teaspoon cinnamon
    1/4 teaspoon nutmeg
    1/2 cup rolled or quick cooking oats
    2 eggs, beaten
    1/4 cup vegetable oil
    1/4 cup dried red currants or golden raisins
    1 1/4 cup milk

Preheat oven to 400 degrees F. Line a muffin tin with papers. In a bowl, sift together flours, baking powder, salt, sugar, and spices, then stir in oats. In a larger bowl, beat eggs with oil to emulsify, then stir in dried fruit. Add milk and gently stir in dry ingredients (do not overmix). Spoon into cups, filling them 1/2 to 3/4 full. Bake at 400 until golden brown (16–18 minutes). Serve warm. Makes 12 muffins.

"Thank you for this opportunity. I've learned some information/ skills to help me be calmer and more at peace. I will be able to help not only myself more but also my husband and our children. You have helped many with this gift."

Pine Nut Pumpkin Bread

If there is a secret to great quick bread, it's fresh baking soda and baking powder. Toss out your old ones every New Year's Day (along with musty old spices and herbs) and you'll discover that fresh leavening makes a positive difference.

> 1 1/4 cup unbleached white flour
> 1 1/4 cup whole wheat pastry flour
> 1 teaspoon baking soda
> 1 teaspoon baking powder
> 1/4 teaspoon salt
> 1/2 cup buttermilk
> 1 organic lemon, juiced, rind grated
> 1/4 cup unsalted butter, softened
> 1/2 cup sugar
> 1/4 cup brown sugar, lightly packed
> 2 large eggs, beaten
> 1 1/4 cup pumpkin pulp (canned works fine)
> 1 cup toasted pine nuts

Preheat oven to 350 degrees F. Butter a large loaf pan, dust with flour, line with waxed paper or parchment, set aside. In a bowl, sift together the flours, baking soda, baking powder, and salt, set aside. Combine buttermilk and lemon juice, set aside. In a large bowl, cream butter with sugars and lemon zest until light. Blend in eggs, pumpkin, and pine nuts. Add flour and milk mixtures in alternating thirds, mixing just enough to blend the batter (it will be lumpy). Fill loaf pan 2/3 full (cook any extra in a small baking dish). Bake at 350 until a toothpick comes out clean (55–60 minutes). Cool the pan on its side for 3 minutes, change sides and repeat. Carefully loosen the loaf and invert onto a cooling rack. Makes 1 loaf.

"One begins deeper healing when one breathes the beauty of Harmony Hill."

Zesty Orange Banana Bread

For a change, use lemon, lime, or tangerine zest and try nutmeg or coriander instead of cardamom.

1 teaspoon butter
1 teaspoon cinnamon
1 cup unbleached white flour
1 cup whole wheat pastry flour
1 teaspoon baking soda
1 teaspoon salt
1/2 teaspoon cardamom
1 organic orange, rind grated
2/3 cup brown sugar, lightly packed
2 large eggs, beaten
3 ripe bananas, mashed
2 teaspoons vanilla

Preheat oven to 350 degrees F. Butter a large loaf pan, dust with cinnamon, set aside. In a bowl, sift together the flours, baking soda, salt, and cardamom, set aside. In another bowl, blend orange rind, brown sugar, eggs, bananas, and vanilla. Add flour mixture, stirring just enough to blend the batter (it will be lumpy). Fill loaf pan and bake at 350 until a toothpick comes out clean (55–60 minutes). Makes 1 loaf.

"How does one put into words the profound spirit of welcoming and wellness that permeates Harmony Hill? The gardens, the labyrinth, the facilities, the food, and above all the staff, all nurture the sense and the soul. I remain centered and balanced two weeks since leaving there."

Double Corn Bread

Sizzling butter in a hot frying pan gives this tender, moist cornbread a super crispy crust. Good additions are cubed cheddar or Pepper Jack cheese, sunflower seeds, or pine nuts.

    2 teaspoons virgin olive oil
    2 teaspoons unsalted butter
    1 cup yellow cornmeal
    1 cup whole wheat pastry flour
    1 tablespoon sugar
    3 teaspoons baking powder
    1 teaspoon salt
    1 egg, lightly beaten
    1 1/4 cup buttermilk
    1 cup corn kernels, fresh or frozen
    1 cup sharp cheddar or Pepper Jack cheese, diced (optional)

Combine oil and butter in a heavy iron frying pan (9–10-inch) and place in the oven, then preheat oven to 400 degrees F. Sift together dry ingredients, set aside. In a mixing bowl, whisk together the egg and the buttermilk. Add dry ingredients and stir until barely mixed (batter is thick). Fold in corn and cheese (if using) and spoon into hot frying pan (butter should bubble up and foam). Bake at 400 until golden (18–20 minutes). Serves 6–8.

Chocolate Hazelnut Bread Pudding

Stale bread can be recycled into crumbs, croutons, or delectable puddings like this one. We like Northwestern hazelnuts in this custardy, sweet pudding, but almonds or pecans work nicely, too.

    4 cups stale whole grain bread, cubed
    1 cup dark chocolate chips or chunks
    1 cup toasted hazelnuts, chopped
    4 cups milk

2 eggs, slightly beaten
1/2 cup Grade B maple syrup or brown sugar
1/4 teaspoon salt
2 teaspoons real vanilla extract

In a baking dish, combine bread, chocolate, and nuts. In a bowl, combine milk, eggs, maple syrup or sugar, salt, and vanilla. Pour over bread and let stand for 10 minutes, pushing bread down with a spoon to get evenly moist. Bake at 350 degrees F until puffed and set (50–60 minutes). Serves at least one.

Savory Cranberry Walnut Bread Pudding

Try a combination of half stale cornbread and half whole grain muffins or bread in this savory side dish, which partners perfectly with roast chicken.

4 cups stale whole grain bread, cubed
1/2 cup dried cranberries
1 cup walnuts, chopped
4 cups milk
2 eggs, slightly beaten
2 cloves garlic, minced or finely chopped
1 teaspoon Worcestershire sauce
1/2 teaspoon Tabasco® sauce
1 teaspoon smoked paprika

In a baking dish, combine bread, cranberries, and walnuts. In a bowl, combine milk, eggs, garlic, sauces, and paprika. Pour over bread and let stand for 10 minutes, pushing bread down with a spoon to get evenly moist. Bake at 350 degrees F until puffed and set (50–60 minutes). Serves 6–8.

"Before the three-day retreat at Harmony Hill, my life had shut down and I was in a deep depression. Now I wake up laughing, grateful that I am still alive."

Harmony Hill Zucchini Bread

This recipe makes two loaves, so share with a friend or freeze one. Zucchini bread is terrific toasted or spread with homemade almond butter.

1/2 teaspoon walnut or safflower oil
1 tablespoons cinnamon
3 cups whole wheat pastry flour
2 teaspoons baking soda
1 teaspoon baking powder
1 teaspoon salt
1 teaspoon coriander or nutmeg
1 organic orange, rind grated
1 cup dark brown sugar, packed
1/2 cup unsalted butter
3 large eggs, lightly beaten
3 teaspoons real vanilla extract
3 cups zucchini, grated (use the food processor)
1 cup walnuts, chopped

Preheat oven to 350 degrees F. Lightly oil 2 bread pans, dust with cinnamon, set aside. Sift together remaining cinnamon, flour, baking soda and baking powder, salt, and coriander, set aside. In a large bowl, rub orange zest into sugar until fragrant (a few seconds), then cream in butter. Stir in eggs completely, then add vanilla, zucchini, and walnuts and blend well. Stir in dry ingredients and spoon batter into oiled pans. Bake at 350 for 50 minutes or until deep golden brown (internal temperature of 200 degrees F). Cool completely before slicing.

Tip To avoid soggy loaves, cool for 5 minutes, turn pans on side and cool for another 5 minutes, then slide loaves out onto a wire cooling rack.

"The retreat provided a way for us to hold the cancer in a different light—not as a problem, but as an opportunity."

French Cheese Bread (Gougère)

Gougère, or French cheese bread, dates back to late Medieval times and one bite tells you why it's still around. Any savory cheese will do in this ravishing bread, from extra sharp cheddar to Swiss, Parmesan, or even Roquefort.

 1 cup water
 1/4 cup unsalted butter
 1/2 teaspoon salt
 1/4 teaspoon freshly ground black pepper
 3/4 cup whole wheat pastry flour
 4 eggs
 3–4 ounces (about 1 cup) hard cheese (Romano, Cheddar),
     coarsely grated, finely diced, or crumbled

Preheat oven to 400 degrees F. In a small saucepan, bring water, butter, salt, and pepper to a boil over medium high heat. Dump in the flour all at once and stir until the dough makes a soft ball (1–2 minutes). Remove from heat and add eggs one at a time, stirring until each is completely incorporated before adding the next. Stir in all but 2 tablespoons cheese and drop by tablespoonfuls onto a rimmed baking sheet.

Begin by making a circle of 7 balls, then build a wreath shape outward, letting each ball of dough barely touch its neighbors. Sprinkle with remaining cheese and bake at 400 degrees F until puffed and golden (40–45 minutes). Serve hot. Serves 6–8.

"Thank you for the opportunity to renew my spirit and to share my journey with other cancer survivors. We are all walking different paths, some are easier than others, but we all ultimately reach the same destination of finding our centered self and living in the moment, not knowing how many moments are left for us."

Our guests always love homemade yeast bread. Double Oat, Rye, Anadama, all are greeted with deep appreciation. Homemade bread toasts beautifully and makes great sandwiches. Leftovers are exceptional in bread pudding and as fresh bread crumbs (grate the heels in the food processor and freeze them for use in meatloaf and similar recipes).

To keep rising bread out of drafts, put it in the oven with the oven light on. The heat from the bulb keeps the oven between 75–85 degrees F, a perfect environment for growing bread.

Although making bread does take time, most of it is time that you can spend doing something else. When you know you'll be home all day, start your bread after breakfast. By lunchtime, it's ready to be kneaded and shaped into loaves (10–15 minutes). In another hour or so, it's ready to bake for 40–50 minutes. Time it to be done close to dinner time: the scent of baking bread is as irresistible as the wholesome result.

Anadama Bread

A traditional New England yeast bread, this makes wonderful sandwiches and toast. It's terrific in bread pudding or stuffing.

> 1 cup yellow cornmeal
> 2 tablespoons unsalted butter
> 1/3 cup molasses
> 2 teaspoons salt
> 1 1/4 teaspoons or 1 packet dry yeast
> 4 1/2 cups bread flour

In a large bowl, combine cornmeal and butter with 2 cups boiling water. Let stand 1 hour. Stir in molasses, salt, and yeast, then blend in 4 cups flour. Let rise in an oiled bowl until doubled (about 2 hours). Knead into 2 loaves (about 5 minutes each), adding remaining flour as needed. Let rise until doubled in bulk (about 1 1/2 hours). Bake at 350 degrees F until done (40–50 minutes, to internal temperature of 180 degrees F). Makes 2 loaves.

No-Knead Double Oat Bread

Adapted from an old fashioned recipe, this is very popular at breakfast, toasted and spread with homemade jam.

    1 cup steel cut oats
    1 cup old fashioned rolled oats (not quick-cooking)
    1 tablespoon butter or canola oil
    1/3 cup dark molasses
    2 teaspoons salt
    1 1/4 teaspoons or 1 packet dry yeast
    2 cups whole wheat pastry flour
    3 cups bread flour

Preheat oven to 350 degrees F. In a large bowl, combine oats, butter or oil, molasses, and salt with 2 cups boiling water. Cover with a plate, let stand for 1 hour. Add yeast and flours and mix well. Let rise in an oiled bowl until doubled in bulk (about 2 hours). Stir well and divide between 2 oiled loaf pans. Let rise again until doubled (about 1 1/2 hours). Bake at 350 until done (40–50 minutes, or to internal temperature of 180 degrees F). Makes 2 loaves.

"Cancer does not choose its victims according to 'ability to pay.' So much of cancer care and treatment, however, does depend on that. Being given care [here at Harmony Hill] at no charge, regardless of 'ability to pay,' works magic for those who cannot pay—and for those who can. Being given, free of charge, the love, respect, and nurturing made me feel worthy. For that reason, I have become a monthly supporter of the Hill."

Ginger Rye Bread

Before the days of prepackaged yeast, cooks used ginger to lighten up rye breads, which can be on the heavy side.

    2 cups buttermilk
    1 tablespoon canola oil
    2 tablespoons brown sugar
    1 tablespoon ground ginger
    1 tablespoon caraway seed
    2 teaspoons salt
    1 1/4 teaspoons or 1 packet dry yeast
    3 cups sifted dark rye flour
    3 cups bread flour

Preheat oven to 350 degrees F. In a large bowl, combine buttermilk with oil, sugar, ginger, caraway seed, salt, and yeast. Stir in rye flour and 2 1/2 cups of bread flour. Let rise in an oiled bowl until doubled in bulk. Shape into 2 loaves, kneading in more flour as needed. Let rise again until almost doubled in bulk (rye bread may not quite double). Bake at 350 until done (40–50 minutes, or to an internal temperature of 180 degrees F). Cool before slicing. Makes 2 loaves.

"Thank you to the donors who made this retreat possible. Even though I'm done with treatment, I'm still processing the cancer experience. Harmony Hill gave me the chance to step back and evaluate that experience and assess my goals with others who are going through the same experience. The retreat helped me to be away from my daily life, so I could really feel my feelings and set meaningful goals."

Nutty Cherry Cream Scones

Pine nuts add a lush, toasty flavor, but you can also use pecans, walnuts, or cashews.

  1 cup whole wheat pastry flour
  1 cup unbleached white flour (plus 2 tablespoons for rolling)
  2 teaspoons baking powder
  2 teaspoons sugar
  1/2 teaspoon salt
  1/4 cup sweet (unsalted) butter
  2 eggs, lightly beaten
  1/2 cup cream
  2 tablespoons toasted pine nuts
  1/4 cup dried tart pie cherries

Preheat oven to 450 degrees F. Sift together dry ingredients. Work in butter to the consistency of coarse corn meal. Add eggs and half the cream, stirring gently, then add remaining cream, 1 tablespoon at a time (you may not need it all), until you have a soft dough that can be handled easily. Add pine nuts and cherries and knead to blend (20–30 seconds). Scatter reserved flour on a flat surface and roll out dough into a rectangle 3/4 inch thick. Cut in a crisscross grid to make 3- to 4-inch long diamonds. Slide scones onto baking sheets and bake at 450 for 12–15 minutes until puffed and lightly golden. Makes about a dozen scones.

"The retreat at Harmony Hill allowed me a space to get away from problems and focus on healing. It nurtured me. I live alone, and it was wonderful to be fed and nourished."

Double Date Breakfast Rolls

Dried dates in the dough and softer ones in the filling make these spicy rolls extra tasty.

1 cup buttermilk or any milk (nonfat works fine)
1 1/4 teaspoons (1 package) dry yeast
1/4 cup sugar
2/3 cup sweet (unsalted) butter, at room temperature
1 teaspoon salt
3 tablespoons organic orange rind, grated (3 oranges)
2 tablespoons dried date bits, chopped
1 cup whole wheat pastry flour
1 1/2 cup unbleached white flour
1/4 cup brown sugar
1 teaspoon cinnamon
1 teaspoon coriander
1/2 teaspoon nutmeg
1/4 cup date pieces (rolled in oat flour)
1/4 cup hazelnuts, toasted and chopped
1 cup confectioner's (powdered) XXX sugar
1/2 teaspoon vanilla
juice of one orange

Heat the milk to lukewarm in the microwave or on the stove top. Add yeast and 1 teaspoon sugar and let work for 5 minutes. Stir in 1/3 cup butter, sugar, and salt, 1 tablespoon grated orange rind, and date bits, then add flour 1/2 cup at a time to make a soft dough you can handle easily (you may not need it all). Knead until smooth, then roll into a rectangle 1/4 inch thick. Spread dough with 2–3 tablespoons butter and sprinkle with remaining grated orange rind, brown sugar, spices, date pieces, and hazelnuts. Roll up lengthwise (like a jellyroll) and cut in 3/4-inch slices. Put the rolls, cut side down, in a buttered baking dish. Cover with a damp towel and let sit until doubled in bulk.

Bake at 350 degrees F until golden brown (about 25 minutes). Blend remaining butter with confectioner's sugar, vanilla, and orange juice (start with 1 tablespoon) to make a thick frosting. Frost rolls when cool and serve. Makes about 12 rolls.

Ginger Orange Scones

These beautiful, fragrant scones make holiday breakfasts especially festive.

1 cup whole wheat pastry flour
1 cup unbleached white flour (plus 2 tablespoons for rolling)
2 teaspoons baking powder
2 teaspoons sugar
1/2 teaspoon salt
1/4 cup sweet (unsalted) butter
2 eggs, lightly beaten
1/2 cup cream
2 tablespoons organic preserved orange peel, chopped
2 tablespoons crystallized ginger, chopped
1/3 cup orange marmalade

Preheat oven to 450 degrees F. Sift together dry ingredients. Work in butter to the consistency of coarse corn meal. Add eggs and half the cream, stirring gently, then add remaining cream, 1 tablespoon at a time (you may not need it all), until you have a soft dough than can be handled easily. Add orange peel and ginger and knead to blend (20–30 seconds). Scatter reserved flour on a flat surface and roll out dough into a rectangle 3/4 inch thick. Cut in a crisscross grid to make 3- to 4-inch long diamonds. Slide scones onto baking sheets and bake at 450 for 12–15 minutes until puffed and lightly golden. Brush immediately with marmalade (easier if you heat it briefly in the microwave). Makes about a dozen scones.

"A mere 'thank you' seems inadequate. For someone who cares for others for a living, it was wonderful to be cared for in such a loving, warm environment."

10 Delicious Desserts

Harmony Hill desserts are hugely popular with our guests, who often ask for our recipes. From Baked Apples to Fresh Blueberry Pie, you'll find a year's worth of delectable treats here.

We base many desserts on seasonal fresh fruit, some of which comes from our beautiful, bountiful gardens. Though a few of the goodies in this chapter are totally indulgent, many of our cookies are wheat- or dairy-free, and our puddings, tarts, and crisps have similar variations to ease dietary difficulties.

Cooking at Harmony Hill

HARMONY HILL FAVORITES

Chocolate Almond Goat
   Cheese Truffles
Harmony Hill Chocolate Pudding
Dark Chocolate Sorbet
Rhubarb Sorbet
Summery Blueberry Cup
Peachy Keen Smoothie

PIES AND COBBLERS

Fresh Blueberry Pie
Raspberry Dream Pie
Spunky Rhubarb Pie
Almond Pie Crust
Gretchen's Banana Dream Pie
Graham Cracker Crust
Harmony Hill Blackberry Cobbler
Almond Nectarine Torte
Lemon Whipped Cream
Lemon Syrup
Huckleberry Angel Pie
Hazelnut Pumpkin Pie

FANCY FRUIT

Fresh Fall Apple Cup
Slow Plums
Baked Apples
Poached Pears with Fig and
   Ginger Sauce
Maple Pears
Apple Hazelnut Upside-Down Cake

COOKIES

Harmony Hill
   Lavender Shortbreads
Coco-Date-Nut Chews
Toasty Oaties
Peanut Wonders
Lemon Ginger Drops
Catalan Panelletes
Cranberry Orange Crisps
Chocolate Cherry Meringues
Almond Crescents

"It is said, 'Someone who saves one life saves the world.' Due to your generosity, many people attend this retreat who would not be able to otherwise. Harmony Hill offers not only tools for coping with cancer, but also a sense of compassion and giving that is innate to its core, feeding the soul. Bless you!"

Chocolate Almond
Goat Cheese Truffles

Sugar-free candy? Oh my yes. Delectable yet guilt-free, these handsome tidbits are delightful for holiday parties or gifts.

> 4 ounces bittersweet chocolate, chopped
> 6 ounces fresh goat cheese (plain)
> 1 teaspoon pure vanilla extract
> 1/4 cup toasted almonds or hazelnuts
>   (see Chapter 1, Appetizers)
> 1/4 cup unsweetened dark cocoa powder

In a heavy saucepan, melt chocolate chips over low heat, stirring often until smooth. Remove from heat and cool for 10 minutes. Cream goat cheese and vanilla, stir in chocolate and almonds. Cover mixture and chill, well-wrapped, until firm (about 1 hour). Shape into 1-inch balls, roll in cocoa powder and serve. Chill for up to 3 days. Makes about 18 truffles.

Harmony Hill Chocolate Pudding

A secret ingredient (tofu) adds extra protein to this creamy and satisfying dessert. Be sure to use silken (boxed) tofu or the texture may be grainy.

> 1 1/2 cups firm silken tofu
> 1/2 cup sugar
> 1/2 cup dark cocoa powder (unsweetened)
> 2 teaspoons real vanilla
> few grains sea salt

Combine in a food processor and puree until smooth. Serve immediately or chill. Serves 4–6.

Dark Chocolate Sorbet

Fat-free, dairy-free, and intensely chocolatey!

    1 cup sugar
    2/3 cup dark unsweetened cocoa powder
    1 1/2 cups water
    1 teaspoon real vanilla
    1–2 tablespoons Kahlua, Fra Angelico, or
        Framboise (optional)

Blend sugar and cocoa powder in a heavy saucepan. Slowly
add 1 1/2 cups water, stirring constantly. Bring to a simmer
over medium heat and cook, stirring, until sugar dissolves
(6–8 minutes). Bring to a boil over high heat and cook, stirring
constantly, until syrup turns thick and glossy (1–2 minutes).
Cool to room temperature, stir in vanilla and liqueur (if using).
Cover and cool in refrigerator for at least an hour. Pour into an
ice cream maker and process according to machine directions or
still-freeze in a tightly covered container. Makes about 2 cups.

Rhubarb Sorbet

Fresh rhubarb is one of spring's most welcome early crops. It
freezes well, so you can enjoy this refreshing dessert any time.
Serve this tart, tangy sorbet topped with fresh strawberries or
blueberries. For the more sophisticated palate, it's also delicious
with roast chicken and shredded fresh basil.

    1 1/2 cups water
    2 organic lemons, juiced, rind grated
    1 1/3 cups sugar
    4 cups (1 pound) rhubarb, chopped in 1-inch pieces

In a deep saucepan, combine water, lemon rind, 1/4 cup lemon
juice, and sugar. Bring to a boil over medium high heat, reduce
heat to medium low, cover pan and simmer until tender (6–8
minutes). In a food processor, puree to a fine slurry. Chill
for 2–3 hours, then freeze in an ice cream maker (or in any
container; just stir with a fork before serving). Freeze until firm
(2–3 hours). Serves 4–6.

Summery Blueberry Cup

Sprightly and summery, this simple little treat tastes fancy
enough for a party.

    1 pint lemon sorbet
    2 cups fresh blueberries
    1/4 cup brown sugar or maple syrup
    2 tablespoons candied ginger, finely chopped

Divide sorbet among four dessert bowls or tall ice cream glasses.
Mash 1/2 cup blueberries with brown sugar or maple syrup and
drizzle over each sorbet. Top with remaining blueberries and
sprinkle with candied ginger. Serve at once. Serves 4.

Peachy Keen Smoothie

Harmony Hill's director, Gretchen, loves to make summer
smoothies like this one from local fresh fruit. This lively
summer smoothie tastes especially good after a long walk on the
Hood Canal beach.

    4 ripe peaches, peeled and chopped
    1 cup raspberries, strawberries, or blackberries
    1 tablespoon mint, finely chopped
    1 quart vanilla yogurt (nonfat works fine)

Combine all ingredients in a food processor or blender and puree
until smooth. Serve immediately. Serves 4–6.

*"I have been surprised. I would recommend the Harmony Hill
program as well as the facilitators to anyone. For a guy who
was just accompanying his wife, and was too dumb to notice,
it's been perfect. I don't have words to convey my gratitude."*

In berry season, Harmony Hill's ovens are full of fragrant fruit pies and cobblers. We freeze plenty of blueberries, blackberries, and peaches so we can enjoy the taste of summer all year round.

Fresh Blueberry Pie

Refreshing on a summery evening, this well-chilled concoction tastes wonderfully light and fresh.

    3/4 cup sugar
    3 tablespoons cornstarch
    1/4 teaspoon freshly grated nutmeg or coriander
    1 organic orange, juiced, rind grated
    1 tablespoon lemon juice
    5–6 cups fresh blueberries
    1 tablespoon butter
    2 teaspoons real vanilla
    1 9-inch pie crust, baked and cooled

In a deep, heavy saucepan, combine sugar, cornstarch, spice, and orange rind. Stir in 2 tablespoons orange juice and lemon juice and cook over medium high heat until mixture thickens and becomes translucent (4–6 minutes). Stir in berries and cook for 2 minutes. Remove from heat and stir in butter and vanilla. Cool to room temperature, pour into pie shell and chill (covered with waxed paper) for 6–8 hours (or overnight). Serves 6–8.

"I feel nourished and content, grateful and amazed. The Harmony Hill retreat center is a place of healing. The journey of cancer requires a multitude of support systems and interventions. The staff and faculty of the center provide tools for living, in a loving and peaceful environment."

Raspberry Dream Pie

Light, lovely, and luscious, this summery dessert is equally good with any soft fruit, from nectarines or apricots to huckleberries or loganberries.

>   1 cup unsweetened coconut flakes or curls
>   1 cup graham cracker crumbs
>   1 cup roasted, unsalted almonds, finely chopped
>   1 tablespoon melted butter
>   4 cups raspberries
>   2 cups vanilla yogurt (nonfat works fine)
>   2–3 tablespoons honey or Grade B maple syrup

In a 350-degree F oven, toast coconut until pale brown (6–8 minutes), set aside. In a pie dish, combine graham cracker crumbs, almonds, and melted butter. Pat evenly over bottom and sides. Layer 1 cup raspberries over the bottom, set aside. In a blender or food processor, combine 2 cups raspberries with yogurt and puree to a thick paste. Season to taste with honey, starting with 2 tablespoons. Spoon filling into pie dish, top with remaining raspberries and sprinkle with toasted coconut. Chill or serve immediately. Serves 6–8.

Spunky Rhubarb Pie

A popular spring favorite! Lively with candied ginger, coriander, and fresh oranges, this zippy confection is delicious served hot or chilled.

>   1 1/2 cups sugar
>   1 teaspoon ginger powder
>   1 teaspoon coriander or nutmeg
>   1/8 teaspoon sea salt (or any)
>   1 organic orange, juiced, rind grated
>   3 tablespoons quick-cooking tapioca
>   5 cups rhubarb, finely chopped
>   1/4 cup candied ginger, chopped
>   1 Almond Pie Crust (see next page)

Preheat oven to 400 degrees F. Sift together the sugar, ginger powder, coriander, and salt, then rub in orange zest with fingers for 10–20 seconds to build fragrance. Stir in tapioca and 1/3 cup orange juice, then gently toss with rhubarb and candied ginger to coat well. Spoon into pie shell and bake at 400 for 20 minutes, reduce heat to 350 degrees F and bake until golden and bubbling (20–25 minutes). Let stand until cool or chill well. Serves 6-8.

Tip Add 1 teaspoon of fresh (or half a teaspoon of dried) lavender flowers to raspberry or blueberry pie.

Almond Pie Crust

Gluten-free and high in protein, this quick crust is great for fruit pies or quick summery tortes. For use with savory fillings, cut the sugar.

   1 cup toasted almonds (see Chapter 1, Appetizers)
   1/3 cup confectioner's sugar
   1/4 teaspoon sea salt
   2 tablespoons unsalted butter (cold)

In a food processor, grind almonds to a fine meal. Add sugar and salt, process for 10 seconds. Add butter a teaspoon at a time, processing for 3–4 seconds between each addition. Pat crust into pie dish (chill dough if too sticky to handle). Fill and bake as directed for pie. To pre-bake, bake at 350 degrees F 12–15 minutes until set and golden. Makes one crust.

"Food was tremendously refreshing and restoring. Every meal here feels like a gift from a loving mother."

Gretchen's Banana Dream Pie

Harmony Hill founder Gretchen Schodde loves this wholesome, not-too-sweet pie after a light evening meal.

   3/4 cup sugar
   5 tablespoons cornstarch
   1 1/2 cup soy or almond milk
   1 tablespoon real vanilla
   1/2 teaspoon salt
   2 tablespoon unsalted butter
   8 ounces firm tofu, chopped
   2 large bananas, sliced
   1 Graham Cracker Crust (see below), cooked and cooled
   1/3 cup toasted almonds, coarsely chopped

In a saucepan, combine sugar and cornstarch, add soy or almond milk, vanilla, and salt and bring to a simmer over medium heat. Cook, stirring, until very thick (4–6 minutes). Chill well (at least an hour).

In a food processor, combine chilled mixture with tofu and process until smooth and creamy (1–2 minutes). Arrange banana slices over cooled crust and top with tofu mixture and sprinkle with almonds. Chill for an hour or more. Serves 8.

Graham Cracker Crust

A daily half-teaspoon of cinnamon helps regulate blood sugar, so add some to your morning cereal, snack time muffins, or bedtime hot chocolate.

   10 graham crackers
   1 teaspoon cinnamon
   1/3 cup unsalted butter

In a food processor, grind crackers to crumbs. Add cinnamon and butter, one teaspoon at a time, processing for 3–4 seconds between additions. Pat into pie dish. Fill and bake or pre-bake: 350 degrees F until golden (about 20 minutes). Makes 1 crust.

Harmony Hill Blackberry Cobbler

Harmony Hill's extensive grounds boast delicious wild blackberries, which make this juicy cobbler a kitchen specialty. Use Marionberries, blueberries, huckleberries, or raspberries for equally succulent results.

5 cups blackberries (or other berries)
1/3 cup sugar
2 cups whole wheat pastry flour or rice flour
4 teaspoons baking powder
1/2 teaspoon salt
1/2 teaspoon coriander, cardamom or nutmeg (optional)
1/2 cup (1 stick) unsalted butter, cold
1/2 cup milk or buttermilk or hazelnut milk

In a baking dish, combine fruit with 1/4 cup sugar and 3 tablespoons flour, toss gently, set aside. Sift together remaining sugar, remaining flour, baking powder, salt, and spice (if using). Cut in butter and work to consistency of coarse meal. Stir in milk a little at a time until mixture makes a soft ball (you may not need it all). Pat dough to 1/4-inch thickness and cover fruit. Cut a few slashes to release steam and bake at 400 degrees F until golden (35–40 minutes). Serve warm. Serves 6.

"Money could not buy this healing humanness. Know that your donation has helped a fellow human being to be healed and nourished. Medicine and treatments may cure the body, but the Harmony Hill retreat helps heal the mind and spirit."

Almond Nectarine Torte

When unexpected company comes, you can make this elegant, scrumptious dessert in a flash. It's also delectable with fresh peaches, pears, or huckleberries.

> 1/4 cup red currant jelly
> 1 Almond Pie Crust, baked and cooled (see page 181)
> 2 ripe nectarines, sliced (about 2 cups)
> Lemon Whipped Cream (see below)

In a glass dish, microwave jelly for 30–45 seconds; spoon evenly into pie shell. Arrange nectarine slices, cover with Lemon Whipped Cream and serve. Serves 6–8.

Lemon Whipped Cream

Clouds of fluffy cream, bright with lemon, make the perfect counterpoint to tart huckleberries or blueberries.

> 1 cup organic heavy cream
> 1/3 cup Lemon Syrup (see below)

Whip cream until stiff and gently fold in cool syrup. Makes about 2 cups.

Lemon Syrup

French restaurants serve this zingy, tart-sweet syrup with espresso or over fresh fruit. It's also wonderful made with orange, grapefruit, tangerine, or lime.

> 1 organic lemon, juiced, rind grated
> 1/4 cup sugar

Combine in a small saucepan, bring to a boil and simmer for 3 minutes. In a microwave, combine in a glass bowl and cook for 3 minutes at 40% power. Makes about 1/3 cup.

"After being here, at Harmony Hill, I am no longer alone."

Huckleberry Angel Pie

Heavenly! The crisp meringue shell cradles ripe fruit (try peaches, nectarines, raspberries, or strawberries, too) under a cloud of whipped cream. For a real treat, use organic cream, but do be careful; it whips to butter very fast.

    parchment paper (for pan)
    4 eggs, divided
    1/4 teaspoon salt
    1/4 teaspoon cream of tartar
    1 cup sugar
    4 cups huckleberries
    1 cup organic heavy cream
    1/2 teaspoon real vanilla

Line a 9-inch pie pan with parchment paper (top and sides—wrinkles don't matter), set aside. In a deep bowl combine egg whites, salt, cream of tartar, and 3/4 cup sugar. Whip until stiff and spread on bottom and sides of pie pan to make a shallow shell. Bake at 275 degrees F for 1 hour or until firm but not brown. Turn off oven and let cool in oven with door closed. When cool, remove parchment paper, fill with fruit and sprinkle with 2–3 teaspoons sugar. Whip cream until stiff, add vanilla and remaining sugar to taste and spread evenly over fruit. Serve immediately. Serves 6–8.

Tip Add 1/2 teaspoon almond or vanilla extract to berry pies for a pleasing change of pace.

"It's been a time for my wife and me to come closer together and also to share the cancer journey with others. Harmony Hill has provided us with tools for health and well-being, tools that we all need."

Hazelnut Pumpkin Pie

Dairy-free Hazelnut Pumpkin Pie is made with hazelnut milk (sold in a box, like soy milk) and zesty fresh ginger. It makes a fabulous dessert for a holiday feast. To make a scrumptious, wheat-free version, use the Almond Crust (page 181).

 1 pie crust
 15 ounces (about 1 3/4 cups) canned pumpkin pulp
 2 eggs, lightly beaten
 1 1/2 cups plain hazelnut milk
 3/4 cup dark brown sugar, lightly packed
 1/2 teaspoon salt
 2 teaspoons ginger
 1 teaspoon cinnamon
 1 teaspoon coriander (optional)
 2 teaspoons real vanilla
 2 tablespoons fresh ginger, peeled and coarsely grated

Preheat oven to 425 degrees F. Press crust into a 9-inch pie pan and crimp edge. Combine remaining ingredients, stirring well. Pour into pie shell and bake 15 minutes at 425. Reduce heat to 350 degrees F and bake for 45 minutes or until pie is done (knife blade comes out clean). Let stand for 30 minutes. Serve warm or cold. Serves 6–8.

"The Harmony Hill program has helped me move beyond the 'medical' treatments and 'cures.' It has done more for my spiritual health than any chemo, radiation, and surgery could come close to! I value my medical treatment, but I love my emotional healing from Harmony Hill."

Fresh Fall Apple Cup

Crisp, sweet, and almost spicy, Honeycrisp and Gala apples don't cook remarkably well, but they are exceptional in fresh desserts like this one.

  2 cups unfiltered apple cider
  2–3 tablespoons honey
  1 tablespoon fresh ginger, grated
  1 teaspoon real vanilla
  2 cups Honeycrisp or Gala apples, cored and diced
  2 tablespoons dried cranberries
  1 pint vanilla ice cream, slightly softened
  1/4 cup toasted almonds

In a saucepan, combine cider, honey, and fresh ginger over medium high heat, bring to a low boil and cook until reduced by half (8–10 minutes). Stir in vanilla, apples, and cranberries, let cool. When sauce is at room temperature, remove half the apples with a slotted spoon (keeping all sauce) and blend drained apples into ice cream. Mound ice cream into individual serving cups and freeze until firm (20–30 minutes). At serving time, drizzle each serving with remaining sauce and top with almonds. Serves 4.

"An invaluable experience that stays with me all year long!"

Slow Plums

The Slow Food movement encourages delicious alternatives to fast food. Sweet-tart, mildly spicy, and intensely delicious, this simple recipe is terrific with Italian prune plums, Santa Rosas, and wild local plums. Newman's Own® organic grape juice is our favorite, but any not-too-sweet kind will do.

2–3 pounds plums, stoned and cut in half lengthwise
1 cup unsweetened grape juice
1 whole clove
1 teaspoon green cardamom pods
1 teaspoon real vanilla

Place plums cut side down on a rimmed baking sheet. Put in a cold oven and bake at 300 degrees F for 40–60 minutes. Fruits should be slightly caramelized on cut side. Combine grape juice, clove, and cardamom pods and boil over medium high heat until juice is reduced by half (5–7 minutes). Add vanilla, remove spices, pour juice over plums and let stand for 5 minutes. Spoon plums over vanilla or ginger ice cream. Can or freeze extras. Makes about 3 cups.

Baked Apples

Washington apples are justly famous and we use them year-round at Harmony Hill. Dessert apples such as Braeburn, Fuji, Pippin, and Pink Lady work well in baked recipes like this one.

4 dessert apples, cored, top inch peeled
1/4 cup dried tart pie cherries
1/2 cup walnuts or pecans, chopped
1/4 cup golden raisins or dried currants
1 organic orange, juiced, rind grated
1 teaspoon cinnamon

Preheat oven to 350 degrees F. Carefully plug bottom hole in each apple with 1–2 dried cherries and place in a baking dish. In a bowl, toss remaining cherries, nuts, raisins, and orange rind and pack (gently but firmly) into apples. Pour orange juice into and over each one and generously dust tops with cinnamon. Bake at 350 until soft (50–60 minutes). Serve warm. Serves 4.

Poached Pears with Fig and Ginger Sauce

A warm and enticingly fragrant finish for an autumnal meal.

> 4 red pears, peeled, halved lengthwise and cored
> 1 cup fresh apple cider (unsweetened)
> 1 tablespoon ginger root, finely chopped
> 1 tablespoon Grade B maple syrup
> 4 ripe figs, quartered lengthwise

In a deep pan, place pears cut side down and add cider, ginger root, and maple syrup. Bring to a boil over medium high heat, cover pan, reduce heat to low and simmer until tender (10–15 minutes). With a slotted spoon, remove pears to 4 dessert plates. Add figs to pan, heat cider to a low boil over medium high heat and reduce to about 1/3 cup (6–8 minutes). Spoon sauce over each pear and serve. Serves 4.

"Thank you all so much. The staff is wonderful. Caring, supportive, very real. It's so uplifting to know there are so many people who care about the health and well-being of people they don't know. You are all amazing, loving people."

Maple Pears

Lush with apple cider and maple syrup, Maple Pears are made magical by green cardamom pods. Common in many cuisines, these plump, fragrant pods are also delicious in rice, quinoa, or black tea.

4 pears, cored and cut in half lengthwise
1 tablespoon canola or walnut oil
1 whole clove
3 green cardamom pods
1 cup apple cider or fresh apple juice
1 tablespoon Grade B maple syrup
1 teaspoon real vanilla

Place pears cut side down on a rimmed baking sheet. Put in a cold oven and bake at 300 degrees F for 40–60 minutes. Fruits should be slightly caramelized on cut side. Combine apple cider or juice, clove, and cardamom pods and boil until juice is reduced by half (5–7 minutes). Discard clove and cardamom, add vanilla and pour juice over pears, then let stand for 5 minutes. Serves 4.

"The labyrinth was life-changing! Entire experience was so life-affirming. This retreat has affirmed my connection to the earth, the universe, and my own body. The life-affirming quality of the experience is helping me both to improve the quality of my life and to heal my body and spirit. Thank you for this most precious gift."

Cooking at Harmony Hill

Apple Hazelnut Upside-Down Cake

Dessert apples like Jonathan or Gravenstein retain texture and flavor well when cooked. This rich, buttery confection makes a pretty party dish.

    1 cup whole wheat pastry flour
    1/2 cup unbleached white flour or barley flour
    2 teaspoons baking powder
    1/4 teaspoon salt
    1/4 teaspoon freshly ground nutmeg
    1/2 cup sugar
    1 egg
    1/2 cup milk
    1/4 cup canola or vegetable oil
    4 tablespoons butter
    1 cup dark brown sugar
    1 cup hazelnuts, chopped
    2 Jonathan or Gravenstein apples, cored and thinly sliced
    1 tablespoon lemon juice
    1/2 teaspoon cinnamon

Preheat oven to 400 degrees F. In a bowl, sift together the flours, baking powder, salt, nutmeg, and sugar, set aside. In a large bowl, stir together the egg, milk, and oil, set aside. In a 10-inch iron (or ovenproof) frying pan, melt butter over medium heat. Sprinkle on brown sugar evenly. Layer on hazelnuts and apples, sprinkle with lemon juice and cinnamon. Stir flour mixture into milk mixture and spoon over apples. Bake at 400 until crisp and golden brown (30–35 minutes). Let stand 5 minutes, then reverse onto a large plate and serve warm. Serves 8.

"It is a joy to realize that what I am going through after all my cancer treatments is typical."

Crisp or chewy, Harmony Hill cookies are some guests' favorite part of the meal! We bake a generous assortment of cookies, some rich and indulgent, others fruit-based and wheat- or sugar-free.

Harmony Hill Lavender Shortbreads

Rich and fragrant, these cookies are like a meditative stroll through Harmony Hill's beautiful Lavender Labyrinth.

> 1/3 cup sugar
> 1 organic lemon, rind grated
> 1/2 cup (1 stick) unsalted butter, softened
> 1 cup unbleached or whole wheat pastry flour or rice flour
> 1/4 teaspoon sea salt
> 1 teaspoon fresh or dried lavender flowers
>   (food grade or organically grown)

In a bowl, rub sugar and lemon rind to bloom fragrance (about 1 minute). Cream in butter, then stir in flour and salt. Work in lavender blossoms, then roll into a 1 1/2 wide log and wrap in waxed paper. Chill until firm (overnight is fine). Slice into 1/4-inch rounds (see Tip below) and place on an ungreased baking sheet. Bake at 350 degrees F until pale golden and set (20–25 minutes). Makes about 2 dozen cookies.

Tip Keep rolled cookies round by sliding the dough into an empty paper towel tube and chilling it for an hour. When slicing, extrude just the amount you are slicing off to avoid flattening the bottom of the roll.

"This retreat has been a life-changing experience. It has turned my fears into something positive. Thank you from the bottom of my heart."

Coco-Date-Nut Chews

These flavorful wheat-free cookies can be frozen and served cold on a hot day.

> 2 cups pitted dates, finely chopped
> 1/4 cup honey
> 1 organic orange, juiced, rind grated
> 1/2 teaspoon real vanilla
> 1 cup pecans or walnuts, chopped
> 1 1/2 cups unsweetened coconut flakes

In a deep, heavy-bottomed saucepan, combine dates, honey, orange juice, and rind and cook, stirring often, over medium heat until thick (5–6 minutes). Remove from heat and stir in vanilla, nuts, and coconut. Cool the dough and roll into 1-inch balls (or use a #40 cookie scoop or melon baller). Makes about 3 dozen cookies.

Toasty Oaties

Though the ingredients are similar to the cookies above, these wheat-free, sugar-free, chewy little treats have a rich, toasty flavor all their own.

> 1 cup rolled oats
> 1 cup shredded unsweetened coconut
> 1 cup almonds or hazelnuts, chopped
> 1 cup pitted dates, chopped
> 1/2 cup golden raisins

Preheat oven to 350 degrees F. Place oats, coconut, and nuts in separate areas on a rimmed baking sheet and bake for 10 minutes. Combine oats and nuts in a food processor with dates and raisins and pulse for 10–20 seconds (mixture will be very coarse). Roll into balls by the tablespoon (or use a #40 cookie scoop or melon baller), then roll in toasted coconut. Makes about 3 dozen cookies.

Peanut Wonders

You'll wonder how these taste so good though they have no flour! These are best made with real peanut butter, the kind that just includes peanuts, salt, and a bit of oil. Good with hazelnut or almond butter, too.

> 1 cup crunchy peanut butter
> 1 cup sugar
> 1 egg

Combine all ingredients well and drop by the teaspoon on a baking sheet. Bake at 350 degrees F until set (15–20 minutes). Makes about 3 dozen cookies.

Lemon Ginger Drops

Spicy and chewy, these flavorful little cookies are perfect after a rich meal or with afternoon tea. For the gluten-intolerant, replace wheat flours with 2 1/3 cups rice flour.

> 1 1/2 cup unbleached flour
> 1 cup whole wheat pastry flour
> 1/4 teaspoon salt
> 3 teaspoons ground ginger
> 1 teaspoon ground cinnamon
> 1 1/2 sticks (3/4 cup) unsalted butter, softened
> 1 organic lemon, rind grated
> 1 cup dark brown sugar, firmly packed
> 1 egg
> 1/4 cup unsulphured molasses

Sift flours, salt, ginger, and cinnamon into a bowl, set aside. In a large bowl, cream butter, lemon rind, and brown sugar, then thoroughly beat in egg and molasses. Stir in dry ingredients in two parts, incorporating well. Drop by the tablespoon (or use a #40 cookie scoop or melon baller) on ungreased baking sheets. Bake at 350 degrees F for 10 minutes (do not overbake). Makes about 4 dozen cookies.

Catalan Panelletes

A Harmony Hill favorite, these lusciously sweet, chewy cookies have a healthy surprise ingredient. Try them once and you'll always bake an extra sweet potato so you can make them often. Parchment paper makes removal to a cooling rack a lot easier (cookies are sticky when hot).

> 1 1/2 cups toasted almonds (see Chapter 1, Snacks and Appetizers)
> 1 1/2 cups unsweetened coconut flakes
> 1/2 cup cooked sweet potato, peeled and mashed
> 1 cup granulated sugar
> 1 egg
> 1 teaspoon real vanilla
> rind of 1 organic lemon, grated
> parchment paper (for baking sheets)

Preheat oven to 350 degrees F. Place coconut on a rimmed baking sheet and bake until lightly golden (6–8 minutes). In a food processor, grind almonds to a coarse meal and combine with coconut. In a large bowl, combine sweet potato, 3/4 cup sugar, the egg, the vanilla, and the lemon rind and stir well. Stir in coconut mixture and chill for at least an hour. Drop by the tablespoon into remaining sugar (use a #40 cookie scoop or melon baller), roll into balls and bake on parchment lined baking sheets at 350 until set but not brown (15–20 minutes). Makes 3–4 dozen cookies.

"Thank you for this safe haven to explore feelings and to learn coping skills, movement, and breathing exercises. The opportunity to stay two nights adds lasting impact—the experience is more likely to stay with me."

Cranberry Orange Crisps

These jewels have chewy centers and crisp edges. For thinner, extra crisp cookies, add 1–2 tablespoons more sugar. These are also delicious with dried tart pie cherries and pecans or pine nuts, as well as with semisweet chocolate chips.

    1 cup unbleached flour
    1 1/4 cups whole wheat pastry flour
    1 teaspoon salt
    1 teaspoon baking soda
    1 cup (2 sticks) butter
    3/4 cup sugar
    3/4 cup dark brown sugar
    1 organic orange, juiced, rind grated
    2 teaspoons real vanilla
    2 eggs
    1 cup rolled oats (old fashioned)
    1 cup dried cranberries

Preheat oven to 375 degrees F. Sift together the flours, salt, and soda, set aside. In a large bowl, cream butter and sugars thoroughly. Stir in orange rind and 1 tablespoon juice, the vanilla, and the eggs. Combine and then add oats and cranberries. Drop by the tablespoon (use a #40 cookie scoop or melon baller) on to ungreased baking sheets and bake at 375 until crisp (10–12 minutes). Makes about 6 dozen cookies.

Chocolate Cherry Meringues

Gluten-free, crisp, and light. If you prefer, use milk chocolate and dried sweet cherries; these cookies taste like heavenly clouds either way.

    2 egg whites, at room temperature
    scant 1/8 teaspoon sea salt
    2/3 cup granulated sugar, sifted
    1/2 teaspoon real vanilla
    2 tablespoons tart dried cherries, finely chopped
    2 tablespoons bittersweet dark chocolate, chopped

Preheat oven to 250 degrees F. Cover two baking sheets with foil or baking parchment. In a deep bowl, combine egg whites and salt and beat with an electric mixer until soft peaks form. Add sugar by the tablespoon, beating constantly between each addition. When egg whites are stiff but not dry, gently fold in vanilla, cherries, and chocolate. Drop by teaspoonfuls on the cookie sheets or pipe into rosettes (use a 1/2-inch star tip). Bake until dry but not browned (45–50 minutes). Turn off oven and leave meringues to cool completely before removing from pan. Store in a tightly sealed tin. Makes about 4 dozen cookies.

Almond Crescents

These meltingly tender Scandinavian classics are traditional treats for the winter holidays.

   1 cup unsalted butter, softened
   1/2 cup sugar
   2/3 cup almonds, ground
   1/4 teaspoon sea salt
   1 cup unbleached flour
   2/3 cup whole wheat pastry flour
   1 cup confectioner's sugar

Cream butter and sugar, stir in nuts, salt, and flours and chill for an hour (overnight is fine). Roll by the teaspoon into slim crescents and bake on ungreased baking sheets at 375 degrees F until pale golden (15 minutes). Cool slightly on racks, then roll in confectioner's sugar and return to racks. Makes about 6 dozen.

"There seem to be very few resources that are warm, nurturing, understanding, and realistic for caregivers and companions. The Harmony Hill retreat is one of a kind."

11 Comfort Food

Our Harmony Hill Cancer Retreats have brought creature comfort and enhanced coping skills to thousands of people whose lives have been touched by cancer. Whether you are a member of this enormous tribe or not, we can suggest some lovely, soothing, comforting foods for the times when you or a loved one needs extra care and coddling.

When the unwell are not able to eat much or often, every bite counts. Unless your doctor orders a restrictive diet, forget the lowfat foods, avoid convenience foods entirely, and concentrate on preparing snacks and small meals based on whole foods. Presentation becomes more important than ever when appetites are depressed, since the sight of too much food can be disturbing. Even normally enticing food smells can destroy uncertain appetites, as can very hot or very cold foods.

To encourage a vanishing appetite, serve convalescent food on a pretty tray, using tiny dishes and smaller utensils. Keep foods separate, and offer just a bite or two of each dish. Try to make sure each meal or snack includes at least 200 calories, and offer 6 to 8 little meals instead of 3 big ones each day.

Freshly squeezed juice, organic whole milk, yogurt smoothies, and even milk shakes are all nutritious snacks, as are popcorn, fresh peanut butter and homemade jam sandwiches, tuna noodle casserole, or mac

SOUPS AND AN OMELET
Soothing Chicken Soup
Ginger Soup with Winter Greens
Avgolemono Soup
Gingered Chicken Soup
Tart Cherry Omelet

SMALL SNACKS AND SOOTHERS
Cinnamon Toast
Warm Apple Sauce
Ginger Tea
Chamomile Calmer
Sleepytime Soother
Italian Hot Chocolate
Restless Night Blues Beaters

and cheese. Chicken soup has been scientifically demonstrated to help heal the common cold and has associative healing properties that make it a classic comfort food.

See Chapter 1, Snacks and Appetizers, for ideas about nutrient-rich snacks, from toasted nuts to deviled eggs. Offer a quarter of a sandwich with a half-cup of soup, a few cherries or half a sliced peach with goat cheese and a few whole grain crackers, or tiny cheese sandwiches made with rye cocktail bread rounds.

When chemo or other strong medications reduce the ability to taste food, appetites can retreat fast. To enhance the flavor of savory food, sprinkle with a little sea salt or nutritional yeast. For sweet or savory liquids, add fresh lemon or lime juice. If sweetness is tolerated best, stir some maple syrup into anything at all.

When taking care of others, it is vitally important that the caregiver also be as well-nourished and as well-rested as possible. Be sure to share the healthy meals and snacks you are offering, and cat nap whenever you get a chance. Walking, swimming, and jogging are all excellent stress reducers, as are singing, laughing, and visiting with close friends. This final chapter of *Cooking at Harmony Hill* contains ideas to help you on your path. May you and all you love be well.

Soothing Chicken Soup

Chicken soup is now scientifically recognized as an effective aid to healing. In cold and flu season, try this wholesome version of the familiar classic.

  10–12 ounces organic skinless, boneless chicken, diced
  1/4 teaspoon rosemary, stemmed and chopped
  1/4 teaspoon kosher or sea salt
  1 organic carrot, shredded
  1 cup fennel, finely chopped
  2 tablespoons jasmine rice
  1/2 teaspoon canola or virgin olive oil
  1 organic lemon, juiced, rind grated
  2 leeks (white and pale green parts only), chopped
  1 tablespoon parsley, chopped

In a large pan, combine chicken with rosemary, 1/8 teaspoon salt, 1/4 of the carrot and fennel, the rice, and 6 cups water. Bring to a boil over medium high heat, reduce heat to low, cover pan and simmer for 20 minutes. Skim off foam, set broth aside.

Meanwhile, in a heavy frying pan over medium high heat, combine oil with lemon zest and leeks. Sprinkle with remaining salt and cook until barely tender (5–6 minutes). Add remaining fennel and carrots, cover and cook for 15 minutes. Add to broth, along with lemon juice to taste (start with 1 tablespoon) and serve, garnished with parsley. Serves 4. Reheats beautifully and keeps in the refrigerator for up to 3 days.

"Thank you for this welcoming, nurturing environment in this time of turmoil and major change. The gift of 'no charge' is incredibly relieving."

Ginger Soup with Winter Greens

A vegetarian version of chicken(less) soup. If texture creates a swallowing problem, puree a cup of this steaming, gingery soup for your convalescent and serve the rest to the family.

1 teaspoon virgin olive oil
6 shallots, thinly sliced
2 inches fresh ginger root, peeled and finely chopped
1 onion, thinly sliced
1/4 teaspoon kosher or sea salt
1 quart vegetable broth
1 bunch spinach, stemmed and shredded
1 bunch red Swiss chard, stemmed and shredded
12 ounces soft tofu, crumbled
1 tablespoon sesame seeds, toasted

In a soup pan, heat oil and shallots over medium high heat and cook, stirring, until barely soft (3–5 minutes). Add ginger and onion, sprinkle with salt and cook, stirring, until barely soft (3–5 minutes). Add broth, bring to a simmer, and add shredded greens and tofu. Cook until greens are barely wilted (3–4 minutes) and serve hot, garnished with sesame seeds. Serves 4.

"This retreat was a great chance for me to begin the emotional journey of dealing with my cancer—my diagnosis is fairly recent [three months]. So it was a great chance for me to begin dealing and processing in a healing, supportive environment. Thank you so much—this was incredible and much needed. Words are hard to find."

Avgolemono Soup

This crowd-pleasing, lemon-infused Greek peasant soup is also ideal for those recuperating from any illness; just add chopped cooked chicken or tofu for additional protein.

> 1 quart chicken or vegetable broth
> 1/4 cup raw basmati or jasmine rice
> 2 organic lemons, juiced, rind grated,
>   or 1/4 cup lemon juice
> 2 eggs, lightly beaten
> 1/4 teaspoon kosher or sea salt
> 1/4 teaspoon freshly ground black pepper
> 2 tablespoons flat Italian parsley, stemmed

In a soup pot, bring broth to a simmer over medium high heat. Add rice and lemon rind (if using), reduce heat to low, cover pan and simmer until rice is tender (20 minutes). Whisk lemon juice into eggs, then add to hot broth while stirring constantly over lowest heat. Add salt and pepper and serve, garnished with parsley. Serves 4.

"I've cried, and I've relaxed. I've explored hidden emotions and I've learned meditative techniques I've so needed.

I am so overwhelmed by the love and support!

'Thanks' is too small a word for this gift. When life as you know it has fallen apart, what a blessing to feel so loved and embraced, so nurtured. Because there is no charge, the gift is greater."

Gingered Chicken Soup

Gingery, spicy soups are more appealing to many folks who can't face heavy or fatty foods.

    1 teaspoon virgin olive oil
    6 cloves garlic, chopped
    3 inches ginger root, peeled and chopped
    1/2 teaspoon chipotle or any hot pepper flakes
    2 stalks celery, chopped
    2 leeks, thinly sliced (white and pale green parts only)
    1/4 teaspoon kosher or sea salt
    1 pound skinless, boneless chicken thighs
        or breasts, chopped
    1 quart chicken broth, hot
    2 tablespoons raw jasmine or basmati rice
    4 cups Black Tuscan kale, finely shredded,
        or 8–12 ounces spinach
    2 green onions, finely chopped

In a soup pot, combine oil with garlic and ginger over medium high heat and cook until soft (2–3 minutes). Add pepper flakes, celery, leeks, and salt and cook for 3 minutes. Add chicken, stir to coat, cover pan and cook until juices run (3–4 minutes). Add broth and hot water to cover if needed (up to 2 cups), cover pan and bring to a boil. Reduce heat to medium low, add rice and simmer until tender (20 minutes). Add greens, stir to wilt (1–2 minutes) and serve, garnished with green onions. Serves 4.

"Healing, harmonious atmosphere. Close to nature. A place of miracles. Wholesome, natural, delicious food. Safe place. Friendly, helpful staff."

Tart Cherry Omelet

This puffy, cheese-enhanced omelet is rather like a savory Dutch Baby, with a tart cherry filling that appeals to those whose taste buds are impaired.

> 4 eggs, lightly beaten
> 1/2 cup fresh ricotta cheese
> 1/4 cup sugar
> 1 can (about 15 ounces) tart pie cherries, drained
>   (save the juice)
> 1 tablespoon corn starch
> 1/4 teaspoon real vanilla
> 2 teaspoons butter
> 1/4 cup sliced almonds, toasted

In a bowl combine eggs, ricotta, and 1 teaspoon sugar and stir until blended, set aside. In a saucepan, bring cherry juice to a simmer over medium high heat. Blend the cornstarch with 1/4 cup cold water and add to the warm juice with remaining sugar (add to taste), stirring constantly until mixture thickens (about 5–7 minutes).

Drain cherries well and add to sauce, stir in vanilla extract, set aside. In a frying pan, heat butter over medium high heat until foamy. Add almonds to cover pan, then gently pour egg mixture over them to fill pan. Cover pan, reduce heat to medium low and cook until puffed and set (2–3 minutes). Spread cherry mixture over half the omelet, fold the other half over the mixture and serve. Serves 4.

"Although I'm the quiet one, I found that hearing the stories all the brave people go through will help me develop inner strength for any or all trials that I face."

Cinnamon Toast

Fragrant and delicious, this childhood favorite is often a successful appetite tempter.

    1 slice whole grain bread
    2–3 teaspoons unsalted butter (soft)
    1 teaspoon sugar
    1/4 teaspoons cinnamon

Lightly toast bread. Cream remaining ingredients, spread generously on bread and lightly toast again until bubbly and golden. Cut in quarters and serve. Serves 1–2.

Warm Apple Sauce

Comforting to a sore throat or an unhappy tummy.

    1 cup unsweetened apple sauce
    1 teaspoon cinnamon or coriander
    1 tablespoon Grade B maple syrup

Combine all ingredients in a glass bowl and warm gently in the microwave (start at 30 seconds). Serve warm. Serves 1–2.

Ginger Tea

Excellent for reducing nausea and increasing an appetite.

    1 tablespoon grated ginger root
    1 tablespoon grade B maple syrup or honey

Bring 2 cups of water to a boil, remove from heat, add remaining ingredients, cover pan and steep for 5 minutes. Strain and serve plain or with honey (if liked). Makes 2 cups.

Chamomile Calmer

Fragrant, calming, and lovely at bedtime.

> 1 tablespoon chamomile flowers or 2 chamomile tea bags
> 3–5 green cardamom pods

Bring 2 cups of water to a boil, remove from heat, add remaining ingredients, cover pan and steep for 5 minutes. Strain and serve plain or with honey (if liked). Makes 2 cups.

Sleepytime Soother

For the lactose-intolerant, make this comforting treat with rice, soy, almond, hazelnut, or oatmeal milk (all are sold in boxes, usually near the powdered milk section). If you choose vanilla-flavored versions of these milk alternatives, just add a few grains of nutmeg, cinnamon, or cardamom.

> 8–12 ounces milk (nonfat works fine)
> 1–3 teaspoons honey or Grade B maple syrup
> 1/4 teaspoon real vanilla or almond extract
> few grains freshly grated nutmeg

Combine ingredients in a mug and heat in the microwave until hot (1–2 minutes). To make in a saucepan, combine milk and sweetener over medium low heat until hot (3–4 minutes). Stir in flavoring(s) and serve. Serves 1.

"My retreat at Harmony Hill was a life-changing event for me. It was a safe place for me to begin to discover my true self, with the warmth and support and wisdom of the staff there to guide me. The beautiful scenery and natural surroundings helped me to feel connected again. I am so grateful that the donations of giving people enabled me to attend."

Italian Hot Chocolate

Italians love the combination of chocolate and hazelnuts, which they call "gianduia." Make your own dairy-free version in minutes, with plain or vanilla-flavored hazelnut milk.

    1 tablespoon water
    1–2 teaspoons dark cocoa powder
    1–3 teaspoons honey or sugar
    1 cup hazelnut milk

Combine water, cocoa powder, and sweetener in a mug and heat in the microwave until hot (about 30 seconds). Stir well, add hazelnut milk and heat again until hot (1–2 minutes). To make in a saucepan, combine water, cocoa powder, and sweetener over medium low heat until hot (1 minute). Stir in milk, heat through and serve. Serves 1.

"I can't imagine anything more perfect. The retreat fed my heart and my soul. Tremendous gratitude, love, and many blessings. We would not have been able to participate without the total generosity of those who made our experience a reality. A life-changing experience—finally, a positive one."

"I feel more empowered now than I have in a long time."

"This is the most healing place I've ever been. The peace, love, and joy enfolds you like a warm blanket. Thank you for providing a beautiful, soulful, healing, joyous retreat. You're a gift! The staff was very, very attentive. Thanks a million for making me feel special!"

Restless Night Blues Beaters

When you can't sleep, nights can seem endless. Here are some suggestions from Harmony Hill Cancer Retreat participants:

Make toast and jam and read Victorian poetry.

Say a "blessing alphabet," working from A-Z, with as many examples for each letter as you can find.

A hot bath with lavender oil.

Hot cinnamon toast and chamomile tea!

Take a 3 a.m. mini-vacation with soothing music, a foot rub, or a gentle face massage with scented lotion.

Sing all your favorite hymns or songs.

Read a Russian novel (it will put you out in minutes).

Other reading suggestions:

"Anything by Jane Austen."
"War and Peace—it's SO DULL!"
"I swear by Shogun—the best part is, it doesn't matter where you start or stop."

Index

C

MORE ABOUT HARMONY HILL

The heart of Harmony Hill's mission is to serve those with a cancer diagnosis and those who love them. We offer these programs without charge to help people facing cancer, and their companions, cope with the physical, emotional, and spiritual challenges of cancer. Our cancer programs serve as supportive adjuncts to medical treatment and do not provide medical care.

Three-day Cancer Retreats. Our primary cancer retreats help individuals find emotional, mental, and spiritual healing in the face of cancer. These retreats offer support and skill-building to help individuals explore the issues, choices, feelings, and concerns associated with a cancer diagnosis.

Tools for the Journey: Living with Cancer. This workshop provides practical resources and strategies for those facing the challenge of cancer. This workshop is available to those on cancer retreat waiting lists or those seeking an introduction to our programs.

Thriving Beyond Cancer. This series of specialized programs on various cancer-related topics serves those who have attended our 3-day cancer retreats and Tools programs. It is also open to those on cancer retreat waiting lists or those seeking an introduction to our programs.

Programs for Cancer Caregivers. These programs are designed to help cancer caregivers cope with the physical, emotional, and spiritual challenges of caring for a loved one with cancer.

Facility Rentals for Groups of All Kinds. Harmony Hill also offers meeting facility rentals for groups of all kinds, including family retreats and celebrations, community groups, organizational renewal, vision clarification, or strategic planning. These rentals provide important revenue to fund our cancer and wellness programs.

Wellness Retreats and Programs. To support the cost-free cancer programs, Harmony Hill offers a range of moderately priced retreats and programs that emphasize individual wellness, stress reduction, and sustainable living.

To donate or to learn more about Harmony Hill Retreat Center and its programs, please visit our beautiful website, **www.harmonyhill.org**, and investigate the many ways in which your life might be enriched.